I0529975

SLAYING VEGAS

Curated by Leigh M. Clark

Aurora Corialis Publishing

Pittsburgh, PA

SLAYING VEGAS

Copyright © 2025 by Leigh M. Clark

All rights reserved. No part of this book may be used, reproduced, stored in a retrieval system, or transmitted by any means—electronic, mechanical, photocopy, microfilm, recording, or otherwise—without written permission from the publisher, except in the case of brief quotations embodied in critical articles or reviews. No part of this book is to be used to train artificial intelligence. For more information, address: cori@auroracorialispublishing.com.

All external reference links utilized in this book have been validated to the best of our ability and are current as of publication.

The publisher and the author make no guarantees concerning the level of success you may experience by following the advice and strategies contained in this book, and you accept the risk that results will differ for each individual.

Neither the authors nor the publisher assumes any responsibility for errors, omissions, or contrary interpretations of the subject matter herein. Any perceived slight of an individual or organization is purely unintentional.

To ensure privacy and confidentiality, some names or other identifying characteristics of the persons included in this book may have been changed. All the personal examples of the authors' own lives and experiences have not been altered.

Printed in the United States of America

Edited by: Renee Picard, Aurora Corialis Publishing

Cover Design: Leigh M. Clark

Paperback ISBN: 978-1-958481-54-7

Ebook ISBN: 978-1-958481-55-4

Table of Contents

Beyond the Neon: What Vegas Taught Me About Grit, Glam, and Showing Up

Most people have a wild story about their first trip to Vegas—mine includes paramedics, blackjack, and a lesson in presence I didn't realize I needed.

I spent my 21st birthday in Las Vegas... with my parents. While my peers were lighting up dorm-room parties, I found myself at a blackjack table with my dad at the Paris Hotel, learning how to play the game—with strategy, patience, and just enough risk to make it interesting. I was soaking in the sparkle of the Strip, feeling both magical and oddly grounding at once.

Spin forward: later that night, my dad woke up feeling ill. I watched paramedics wheel him out of our room—and suddenly the city felt less neon-than-lifeline. My mom and I spent the rest of the week at the hospital, navigating hospital gowns, stale hotel coffee, and the jarring contrast between fantasy and real life.

He recovered. And so did I. But I stayed curious.

That week changed me. Without the usual distractions pulling at my wrist, I finally looked around. Beneath the lights I saw a city of reinvention and drive. A city held together by the caregivers, creatives, and connectors you don't always notice: the overnight nurse, the concierge who remembers your name, the housekeeper who still folds towels into swans after a grueling shift.

Years later, when Vegas called again—for sales conferences—I was not the party girl stumbling home. I was the early morning walker, lacing up sneakers at six a.m., tracing quiet casinos, storefront windows still shuttered, feeling the heartbeat of the city in its softest hours. That slower, softer version of Vegas? It stuck with me.

The Vision: A Book About the Women Building Vegas

Because when the concept of Slaying Vegas came to me, it felt personal: this city is more than escape. It's a place to build. And the women in this book? They're doing that daily—with sparkle and substance.

These are women reinventing the worlds of journalism, PR, lifestyle branding, hospitality, wine, wellness, beauty, and entertainment. Women who have grown bold personal brands with integrity and elegance. Women who bring both grit and glam to everything they touch. Their industries may differ, but their energy is shared: visionary, generous, and endlessly inspiring.

Women Entrepreneurs Lighting Up Las Vegas

According to the U.S. Census Bureau, about twenty-two point four percent of businesses in the Las Vegas–Henderson–Paradise metro area are owned by women—over eighty-three hundred companies, employing more than seventy thousand people, and generating upwards of five billion dollars in revenue. That puts Vegas among the top U.S. cities for women-led businesses.

Across tech, hospitality, design, and service industries, you'll find founders creating not only revenue, but ripple effects. And what's remarkable is that so many of them collaborate—lifting each other up, cross-promoting, and making introductions that change the trajectory of someone else's business.

A Creative Ecosystem: The Arts District & Downtown

In the Arts District in downtown Las Vegas, murals meet movement. Women run vintage boutiques, art studios, bakeries, event collectives, and entire storefront blocks. They host pop-ups and paint nights, community clean-ups and charity auctions. From First Friday festivals to open-mic nights, the creative pulse here is powered by women who have learned how to thrive through expression—and invite others to do the same.

And it's not just art—it's economic revitalization. In just a few years, dozens of new female-founded businesses have opened in the downtown corridor, making it one of the most dynamic areas in the city.

Hollywood's Footprint & Entertainment Expansion

Las Vegas isn't just hosting the stars—it's growing its own constellation. The expansion of the entertainment industry into Vegas is opening up opportunities for producers, stylists, publicists, creative directors, and entrepreneurs who know how to harness storytelling, audience, and experience.

Women are running showrooms, managing talent, launching content studios, and consulting for some of the Strip's most iconic brands. They're doing this while building families, mentoring other women, and staying deeply rooted in community.

Venues like the Smith Center serve as cultural anchors, and women are at the helm—curating seasons, running outreach programs, and shaping the city's cultural future.

Sports City: A New Era of Empowerment

Las Vegas has arrived as a major sports city—and women are playing a key role in shaping that identity.

From the Las Vegas Aces winning back-to-back WNBA championships to the Golden Knights bringing home the Stanley Cup, the city is home to champions—and to the women helping fuel that success behind the scenes.

Whether it's in sports medicine, PR, community engagement, philanthropy, or operations, women are setting a new standard for leadership and impact across athletics.

And with teams like the Raiders, the A's on the way, and the buzz of potential NBA expansion, the sports economy is booming—and women are showing up in every layer of it.

Community at the Core

At the center of all this growth? Heart.

Vegas women don't just work—they connect. They host brunches, run panels, lead support groups, and form masterminds. They help each other get through divorce, burnout, and big, beautiful pivots. They care about what happens in their neighborhoods, and they put their dollars and energy into making those neighborhoods stronger.

This isn't about becoming an influencer—it's about becoming a force.

They're opening coworking spaces with child care. Launching studios where wellness meets activism. Building networking groups where competition doesn't exist—because collaboration is the whole point.

Vegas has always been about reinvention. These women are showing what happens when that reinvention is done with community in mind.

Why This Book Matters

This isn't just about celebrating Vegas. It's about amplifying the energy here—the possibilities.

These women are not background players. They are architects of culture, commerce, and community. They remind us that Las Vegas isn't just a city to visit—it's a city to build in. To grow in. To be seen in.

And most of all, they remind us that it's never too late to rewrite your story.

In Closing

If Vegas taught me anything in the time I spent there, it's that life doesn't stop when the lights dim. It continues—quietly, powerfully—through the people who care. Through the women who serve, show up, and build anyway. Through the stories we choose to tell.

To the women slaying Vegas: you are the show, the strategy, and the soul of this city.

And it's my honor to help tell the story of Vegas—and the women who comprise it.

Lights, Camera, Community
The Real Reason Vegas Sparkles

Rachel Smith

Harnessed high atop a building in Salzburg, Austria, the film crew asked if I was ready.

Ready for what, you might ask?

Ready to duplicate a stunt performed by Tom Cruise in one of his action films.

It had been raining that morning, and the rooftop was slippery, making this a not so "mission possible." But who wouldn't seize the opportunity to jump from building-to-building a la Cruise, so I went for it!

Looking more like Sandy Duncan in Peter Pan than Tom Cruise, it wasn't the sexiest stunt of all time, but I made the jump successfully, nonetheless.

Who would have thought pursuing a career in journalism would land me (literally) in my own amazing movie moment, but it was just one of many surreal situations I would find myself in during my twenty-year career as an entertainment TV host.

It all started with an unexpected call.

"Vegas?! I've been offered an anchor job in Las Vegas?"

All I knew of the city was celebrating on girls' trips, bachelorette parties, and that my Aunt Sherri was once a showgirl in Hallelujah Hollywood at the MGM!

I never thought this could become a community I would cherish and a place I would be proud to call home longer than any other address.

What you quickly learn living here is this is not "Sin City;" it's a terrific town built on kindness, connection, and opportunity.

As a TV host, I have had a front row seat to all the city's exciting transformations while actually evolving myself.

For fifteen years, I hosted two daily entertainment shows on FOX5, covering all the biggest celebrity stories, breaking exclusives on Vegas shows and headliners, and watching "THE Entertainment Capital of the World" truly earn that distinction.

From seeing Shania Twain lead a stampede down the Strip to Caesars to announce her residency, to a headliner who was not "horsing around" when she had to cancel her show just hours before opening night. (We still adore Adele and witnessed a record-breaking production that would make the Rat Pack proud!)

Reporting on these iconic events has been a privilege I don't take for granted.

The highs have been very high: traveling the world to attend premieres and interview A-list stars. I mean from Salzburg to Sevilla, Rio to Rome, Hawaii to Hong Kong, I have covered incredible assignments and had experiences I could only have dreamed of growing up in a small Idaho town.

We couldn't afford fancy vacations, and I only got a passport as an adult after landing my first overseas assignment, so these "pinch-me" moments are always a source of profound gratitude. But behind the glitz and glam are quiet hardships that don't light up any marquee or make front-page news—until they do.

During the pandemic, when the world and certainly Vegas came to a halt, my cherished career also went dark thanks to layoffs.

Pivot? Oh yeah, starting over in your forties sounded as much fun as a long run during a hot Vegas summer. They say challenges build character, but I was not longing for a life lesson; I needed my livelihood.

I wondered, How would I rebuild? Could I redefine my career and my future?

Well, what better place than Vegas to go "all-in" and bet on yourself!

Yep, I doubled down on a decision to turn misfortune into opportunity and try to do this on my own. Create something new on my own terms, trusting that my experience, relationships, and plain old determination and work ethic would deliver a winning hand.

Thankfully, this community came together for so many like me who were not about to fold and were ready to start again.

Vegas is now thriving more than ever, and I have been able to launch my own show, cover Vegas for E! News, take on exciting new projects, and celebrate some full circle moments like interviewing Tom Cruise again at the New York premiere of his latest Mission Impossible.

I have even been traveling globally again, covering dream assignments like the premiere of Emily in Paris—in Paris!

While we have our own Eiffel Tower in Vegas, being able to sparkle after setbacks is the headline I want to not only write for myself but for the wonderful women who shine brightly despite each obstacle.

The women who you will read about in this book will inspire you with their strength, talent, tenacity, and grace—they are SLAYING VEGAS on their own terms in their own impressive ways.

My entire career has been about storytelling, mostly interviewing stars who appear in our favorite films, write our favorite songs, and dazzle us on the Vegas Strip. It is an exciting profession that has been an honor, and one I still immensely love.

Being part of a project, though, where the unsung stars of our city get top-billing is a real thrill—as these are the women who help define what Vegas is all about.

It's a city with bright lights but even brighter people who make living here truly like hitting the jackpot.

As Elvis Presley once said, "All you need's a strong heart and a nerve of steel. Viva Las Vegas!"

*And Viva to the Las Vegas women who exemplify that saying every day.

About Rachel

Rachel Smith is a three-time Emmy Award-winning TV host who has been an anchor in Las Vegas for more than twenty years. She's a contributor for the NBC station in Vegas, KTLA in Los Angeles, E! News, and The Advocate.

As a film critic and voting member of the Critics Choice Association, she has covered every major movie event along with the Toronto, Sundance, and Cannes Film Festivals. She is also on the board of the women's committee and helped create the Seal of Female Empowerment in Entertainment (SOFEE), honoring movies and TV shows that focus on female empowerment.

She is actively involved in the local community and was named one of VEGAS Magazine's "Eight
Most Influential Women" for her charitable work.

Rachel has long advocated for Best Buddies and has been a "buddy" to a young girl with Down syndrome for fifteen years.

She is also a board member of Imagine Dragons' charity, The Tyler Robinson Foundation, which helps pediatric cancer families, and was honored by the Grammy-winning band for her support with their first-ever Legacy Award.

Instagram: @RachelSmithVegas

The Mission After the Miracle - Finding Purpose Through Pain and a Calling to Restore Hope

Krystal Bane

Life doesn't send warnings. It shapes us quietly, through pressure, heartbreak, and unexpected detours. Somewhere in that tension, something beautiful begins to take form. At five years old, packing up boxes with my mom in Concord, Ca., bound for Las Vegas, I had no idea I was stepping into a fire that would both refine and define me.

From the moment I could walk, I moved with intention—first through ballet, tap, and pointe shoes, and eventually onto spring floors and cheer mats. Cheer was more than a sport to me—it was a battlefield of discipline. Every routine built character. By senior year, I captained both my varsity and competitive teams. I led hard, trained harder, and earned every win.

College brought new arenas. At the University of Nevada, Las Vegas, I balanced collegiate cheer, a full course load, and a demanding job at one of the flagship restaurants of a well-known celebrity chef. It was exhausting, but it sharpened my work ethic and taught me poise, perseverance, and the kind of self-reliance my mom had always modeled.

Just before my twenty-second birthday, life took a sharp turn. At a hotel party with old friends, I reconnected with Will, someone I had known since middle school. He seemed refined now, grounded, and carried himself with quiet confidence. Something shifted. Deep conversations followed. Laughter lingered longer. An unspoken love began to grow.

And then, I found a lump.

It rested beneath my collarbone, painless and deceptive. I brushed it off—probably stress. But then came night sweats, relentless fatigue, and a flu-like haze that didn't fade. I avoided the truth as long as I could, until one night over dinner with my mom, Will finally said what I couldn't: "Krystal has a lump in her neck. I think she should get it checked out."

My mom's eyes found mine, and I knew escape wasn't an option. Everything changed in an instant. ER. Bloodwork. Scans. A biopsy. Then the words: Hodgkin lymphoma.

Time fractured. The room fell silent, as if the air had been sucked out. My mother collapsed into a chair. My grandmother was motionless, lost in the weight of the moment. The lights buzzed overhead, the machines beeped in slow motion like storm sirens before impact. And in that cold hospital room, something stirred inside me. Not fear. Fight. I looked my doctor in the eye and said, "Tell me what I have to do."

The tests revealed stage 2B. The cancer had spread from my neck to my chest. Twelve rounds of chemotherapy lay ahead. A port was surgically implanted in my body to receive the drugs. While my survival rate was high, doctors warned the chemo could destroy my ability to have children. That news shattered me. Freezing my eggs wasn't an option I could afford. I walked out of the clinic heavy-hearted, but I clung to one truth: God has a plan. He must.

Then came the conversation with Will. Even when I gave him every reason to walk away—chemo, infertility, baldness, uncertainty—he said one word: "No." He looked at me, steady and unwavering, and said, "Cancer doesn't scare me. If that's the only reason to walk, then I'm staying." In that moment, he became my anchor in the fiercest season of my life. And for the first time, I allowed someone to love me not at my best—but at my lowest. And *that* takes its own kind of strength.

Chemo was brutal and relentless. Day one began with a four-inch needle piercing my chest like a dagger, then hours in a cold chair as poison slowly dripped into my body. I was the youngest patient by decades. Seniors surrounded me in the chemo room, their eyes holding solemn sympathy.

To limit unnecessary exposure during treatment, I applied for an office job at corporate. Within days, I transitioned into my role as sales manager, where I began my love affair with event planning and sales...skills that would inevitably shape my future.

Meanwhile, the chemo took its toll. Week after week, I waged war against my body. My skin slowly turned gray, my reflection became unrecognizable, and my hair fell in clumps. One night, surrounded by friends, we faced the hair loss together. With shaky hands and tear-filled eyes, they helped me shave off what remained. It was crushing—and strangely beautiful; a moment that marked us all.

And then came the words I'd fought to hear. After six months and twelve grueling rounds of chemo, my doctor extended a handshake and said with a knowing smile, "Krystal, your scans are clear. You're done. You're free to go." In that moment, the chains fell. I walked out of that room changed—no longer just a survivor, but a woman on a mission. I had stared down a reality that many don't make it through, and I refused to waste the gift of survival.

As if to remind me He wasn't finished, God brought Jillian into my life.

She was just three, with bright eyes and an infectious giggle. Diagnosed with stage 4 neuroblastoma and given a thirty percent survival rate. But to me, she wasn't a statistic. She was a fighter. I felt an irresistible pull. Maybe it was the survivor in me yearning to seek the survivor in her. Mentoring her wasn't a choice; it was a divine calling.

During my recovery, part of my job was to help organize a major fundraiser for an international nonprofit that grants wishes to critically ill children. My boss shared my story with their CEO, who realized one of the wish recipients—Jillian—was a close friend of mine. Moved by our bond and shared journey, the CEO invited us to speak at the event as honored guests. It wasn't a coincidence, it was fate.

A week later, that same nonprofit offered me a job. I left my beloved corporate career behind and stepped fully into mission-driven work. What began as a job became a greater assignment. I fundraised with everything I had. I helped kids with life-threatening medical conditions find a moment of joy, a memory of hope.

That same year, at a gala benefitting Jillian and her foundation, Will proposed.

We married that September. A year later, our miracle baby, Jaxon, was born—proof that God writes the final chapter.

And Jillian? She defied all odds. Today, she's a cancer-free high schooler, using her story to light up every room she walks into—just like she once lit a flame in me.

I used to think leadership lived on the cheer mat or in a corner office. But real strength rises in hospital rooms, in tearful prayers, or holding the hand of a child fighting for her life. Strength doesn't always roar; sometimes, it whispers when we feel most empty.

Eventually, I stepped away from the nonprofit space to focus on motherhood. Capri, our beautiful daughter, was born soon after. Though deep down, I knew my passion hadn't dimmed.

During the pandemic, my childhood church launched a nonprofit food pantry: Hope For The City. As I watched their impact grow, something sparked. This wasn't a new purpose, but the next level of it. I began volunteering at their holiday event, Hope For Kids, which served 10,000+ children with food, hygiene, clothing, and toys. This wasn't charity—it was a powerful message to each family: *We see you. We believe in you. You are worthy of joy.*

Weeks later, the senior pastor—a longtime family friend— called. He'd heard about my background.

"I think you're exactly who we need," he said.

From that moment on, I've poured myself into the work I was created for.

Since then, Hope For The City has grown into something rare and transformative. We don't offer quick fixes; only lasting solutions. To date, we've served more than thirty million meals. We support over one hundred thousand children annually with critical resources. Our twenty-four/seven Hope Line answers over eighty thousand calls a year to people in crisis. Over four thousand suicides have been prevented through this line alone.

These aren't statistics, they're living proof that when compassion meets strategy, the cycle of poverty can be broken. Our impact has been both humbling and extraordinary.

Someone once asked me a question that stuck with me. Now I'll ask you: What if your breaking point isn't the end, but an invitation to something new?

You don't need to have it all figured out. You just need the courage to keep moving. Let the struggle shape you, not silence you. The world doesn't need perfect people. It needs honest people who rise, scars and all, and turn their pain into passion.

I never expected a lump in my neck to spark a shift in my life's direction. But purpose doesn't always begin with clarity—it often starts with disruption. Every scar, setback, and silent prayer became part of a path I didn't fully understand at the time. Now, I stand in that truth—grateful, grounded, and still growing.

Today, I wear many titles—believer, survivor, daughter, sister, mother, wife—but more than anything, I am a woman called to fight for hope. Not the kind that simply helps us endure, but the kind that restores. The kind that brings dignity to the broken, food to the hungry, and breathes possibility into people who've forgotten how to dream.

I carry my story like a torch—lit by grace, fueled by grit and unwavering faith in a love that moves, heals, and rewrites destinies. This isn't just my journey, it's my legacy.

About Krystal

Krystal Bane is a cancer survivor, nonprofit executive, and purpose-driven leader committed to restoring dignity through service. Raised in Las Vegas by a strong and faith-filled single mother, Krystal grew up shaped by resilience, grit, and a deep sense of responsibility. Her ambition surfaced early, balancing competitive cheerleading, college, work, and leadership roles with relentless determination.

At just twenty-two, her life was interrupted by a diagnosis of stage 2 Hodgkin lymphoma. Chemotherapy threatened her future—including her ability to become a mother—but it did not take away her hope. With the steadfast support of her now-husband, Will, she endured twelve grueling rounds of treatment and emerged cancer-free, vowing to live a life of impact and intention.

Her calling became undeniable when she met Jillian, a courageous three-year-old battling stage 4 neuroblastoma. Their bond opened doors to speaking platforms, fundraising campaigns, and ultimately a full-time career in the nonprofit sector—where survival evolved into service.

Krystal not only beat the odds—she redefined them. Today, she and Will are raising their two beautiful children, living proof of the miracles born from faith and perseverance.

Under Krystal's leadership, Hope For The City has expanded its reach—delivering over thirty million meals, serving more than one hundred thousand children annually, and strengthening mental health initiatives through a twenty-four/seven Hope Line that has helped prevent over four thousand suicides.

She carries her story not as a weight, but as a torch—igniting hope, purpose, and action. Her life is a testament to what's possible when pain is transformed into purpose and compassion becomes a mission.

www.hopeforthecity.org
Instagram: @krystalbane

Valley Views: Finding my Purpose in Hospitality

Amanda Joy Christensen

"Our philosophy has been to take most of the money we would have spent on paid advertising and invest it into customer service and the customer experience instead, letting our customers do the marketing for us through word of mouth." - Tony Hsieh, CEO of Zappos

I was two days away from turning twenty-one years old when I was dropped off at UNLV's campus on a chilly January evening in 2010. I remember staring off into the distance at the MGM Grand, once just a backdrop from my favorite TV show, *CSI*. The campus doors were locked, so I took a cab up to Las Vegas Blvd and checked in to what was my first home in this golden city. I walked into a world of majestic lions in cages, the iconic Studio 54 and Rainforest Cafe, all memories only my mind can remind me of. That night was burned into my mind as I won my first fifty dollars on a slot machine and sipped champagne, wondering what happens next? Was this going to be my new life, would I be disciplined and focused enough to make it in a city where many can't learn how to survive?

Living in Las Vegas was always a series of unforgettable nights, mixed with non-stop music, thrilling energy, and countless "Is this real life?" moments. Iconic, once-in-a-lifetime experiences coming to life from the minds of courageous dreamers—that's the energy that keeps me here always looking for the next big chance. In those rare, raw, glittering, golden nights of putting together once in a lifetime hotel or restaurant experiences, I found my heart's mission: the world of hospitality.

My first project at UNLV was helping coordinate A Night in Sonoma, the annual chef's artist dinner, the proceeds of which went to support the UNLV Hotel College students. It wasn't glamorous inside the hotel's mock kitchen and ballroom, but it was mine. One of the other students—now my husband and the father of my two beautiful children—remembers the way I managed a guest list of over a hundred names using nothing but numbered Post-It notes. I processed credit cards manually, made sure everyone had a seat, and welcomed some of the biggest names in Vegas: the Wynns, the Goodmans, the Adelsons, the Fertitas, and the Tarkanians. These names have truly contributed to the success of the community, each leaving a mark, a legacy.

That night, I learned something far more valuable than how to host a dinner: I learned it's not about the job you have—it's about how you make people feel. That's what hospitality really is. It's not a title. It's a personalized connection.

Throughout the years in Las Vegas, I held many jobs, including serving, working the front desk, hotel sales, special events, revenue management, and answering telephone calls in PBX. I would say yes to anything I could do, as my longing to learn and gain real experience far outweighed the boredom I felt just wondering. I never expected that my career would take me into rooms with visionaries like Tony Hsieh of Zappos, Derek Stevens of Circa, and Jonathan Jossel at the Plaza. Downtown Las Vegas in the 2010s felt like a creative revolution—a collective reinvention of what Vegas could be and still should be. Between the Fremont East District's boom, the Life Is Beautiful Festival, and Zappos' HQ revitalization in tandem with revitalization of the Classic Casinos, there was an energy in the air that was magnetic, collaborative, and alive. The timing of the revitalization happened as the City of Las Vegas took a leap and welcomed eclectic building-sized artwork, and opened many boutique and eye-catching concepts. It brought a totally new blend of authentic art and culture exclusive to our community, that we desperately needed and loved to see brought to downtown. The years I worked downtown here during that era is a time that cannot be replicated. The culture, the camaraderie, and the unity of that decade was lightning in a bottle.

Primarily a global gaming destination, the transformation of Las Vegas into a music mecca of outdoor festivals like Life is

Beautiful, Route 91, Big Blues Bender, Rockin Rio, and Electric Daisy Carnival broke ground on an entirely new music experience travelers sought to discover. It was wonderful to be a part of this shift and offer my guests a completely different Las Vegas experience. I felt like every day I woke up to work in this city, I was bringing a light to anyone I had a chance to serve. The dedication I have to this city, which demanded and refined my skills of hospitality, humility, and hard work was the biggest blessing in my life. The rewards that dedication to serving other beings brings is a love affair unlike any other.

I worked hard—harder than most—but it never felt like enough. I was always close to recognition, but never chosen. I stood out too much to blend in, but not enough to be celebrated. Vegas has a way of making you feel like you're almost there—nearly seen, nearly valued. I spent years pouring myself into jobs that weren't built to keep me. Roles that were transactional. Titles that changed with management. Loyalty that was met with silence when I needed it most. With each heartbreak and disappointment, I used it as the primary stepping stone that shaped my purpose more clearly than success ever could.

When the pandemic hit in 2020, The Strip went dark. I will never forget the eerie silence—no tourists, no music, no buzz. A half-million hospitality professionals were suddenly out of work. In a city where your job title, social image, and status matter more than your story. The shutdowns exposed how fragile and one-dimensional many lives had become, including my own. Without the roles to play, the suits to wear, or the bars to pour into, I realized something: you can't bet your future on someone else's dream.

In November of 2024, I launched my podcast, *Valley Views*—but the truth is, the stories started decades before as I built my career. I saw a need to create a place for anyone to come, share their story and create a new "viewpoint" for someone to learn about Las Vegas. *Valley Views* is this space not just for myself, but for others like me: the behind-the-scenes people, the ones who serve, who care, who invest and who feel. I wanted to create something real. A place where people could find emotional, raw, and authentic insight into what hospitality really means—the kind you won't find in a casino's marketing campaign.

Las Vegas loves its billion-dollar backdrops and bright lights. But who tells the story of the people behind the scenes? Who speaks for the hospitality professionals, small businesses, entrepreneurs, hosts, concierges, and local leadership who carry the emotional weight of a city built on fleeting moments?

They are not paid influencers.

They are not chasing clout.

They are real storytellers.

They are the heartbeat of this city.

Now, as someone wiser and more grounded than the twentysomething, starry-eyed woman I was when I first arrived, I see my purpose more clearly. *Valley Views* is not just a podcast, but a growing community that offers insight, mentorship, and guidance to the next legacy of leaders. A place for those who give so much of themselves—physically, emotionally, and spiritually—to the hospitality industry.

To be a voice in my Vegas Valley was a dream I envisioned when I arrived on the ground in 2010. I felt the magic, the force, the piece of history my two feet were meant to create. Leaving a legacy of stories behind is the oldest tradition in honoring and teaching the next generation how to be something bigger than themselves.

To my children Deryk & Darya, know that even when I'm gone, my stories of hospitality, love, and family are here to inspire you. May you always find hope and faith and brave the unknown, because the biggest dreams are born in the places you least expected. To my mom, Antonette, thank you for buying me the one-way ticket to Las Vegas; it was the best decision you ever made. Without it, I never would have made it!

About Amanda

Amanda Joy Christensen is a hospitality professional, storyteller, and creator of the Vegas-based podcast, *Valley Views*. With over twenty years of experience across nearly every facet of the hospitality industry, Amanda has become a voice for the unsung heroes who power the city behind the scenes.

Her journey began in 2010, when she arrived at UNLV with no clear path, just a hunger to understand true hospitality. Her first UNLV hosted event, A Night in Sonoma, taught her the core of it all: it's not about the job—it's about how you make people feel.

Since then, Amanda has worked alongside legends and visionaries during the downtown Las Vegas renaissance. Her experiences taught her both the beauty and burnout of an industry that often demands everything and can give very little in return. The 2020 shutdown was a turning point that revealed how fragile the illusion of status can be—and clarified her mission to serve with a deeper purpose.

In 2024, Amanda launched *Valley Views*, a podcast within the community honoring the voices of hospitality: creators, caregivers, small business owners, and culture-shapers. It's a legacy project born of hard-earned wisdom, emotional grit, and unwavering belief in serving people the honorable way. In 2025, Amanda was nominated for Forbes Entrepreneur of Impact, among small business innovators leading the next generation of legacy leaders.

Currently Amanda is honored to sit in the room alongside the most dynamic, innovative team of hospitality professionals creating and designing the Otonomus Hotel Las Vegas (O-KEE). The project is a live development of AI-powered systems to help design a new hospitality experience to foster connection, personalization, and service excellence.

Instagram: @amandajoychristensen & @valley.views.podcast
LinkedIn : Amanda Joy Christensen
Valley Views on Spotify: https://bit.ly/4kAcsmB

A Love Letter to the Woman I Once Was

Anoushka Dannin

Dear Me,

You didn't know it then, but all those neutral colored clothes weren't just washing you out—they were slowly convincing you that your glow was gone.

Before motherhood, you took pride in your style. You walked into the office in fun shoes and head-turning outfits, and people noticed. Not because you were trying too hard, but because it was you. Expressive. Confident. Lit up from the inside.

Then life shifted. You left the office and stepped into full-time motherhood. And while it was exactly what was needed and wanted, it also came with changes you didn't fully expect. Your world got louder, your schedule revolved around everyone else, and your style got quieter. Ease and comfort became the priority. Neutrals became the default. Somewhere along the way, you started to fade.

Your relationship with money shifted, too. You had always been independent, and there was a quiet identity loss in not having your own income anymore. You weren't just trying to figure out how to feel like yourself in your style again—you were trying to remember who you were outside of the roles you filled every day.

You were still showing up. You were still taking care of your boys. But you weren't really seeing yourself. Even when you started posting on Instagram as a creative outlet, it felt like a version of you filtered through expectation. You never posted without editing or a filter, because the raw image didn't feel quite right. Remember your cousin's wedding-turned-vacation in Croatia? That should've been magic, but when you look back, the photos feel distant. Every memory blurred by a Snapchat filter. You were capturing moments, but not really present in them, because you weren't fully connected to the woman in the frame.

That was the start of many moments that left you feeling so empty while your life was so full. You didn't want to keep hiding behind the digital polish. You wanted to feel beautiful again—not for anyone else, but for you. That's when you found the beginning of the trail that would lead you home.

You didn't start by changing your wardrobe. You started by changing what was underneath it.

You said yes to an opportunity to partner with a clean, anti-aging beauty brand. You weren't trying to build an empire. You just wanted to feel like you had something that was yours. Something that could grow. Something that could spark joy and maybe—just maybe—bring in an income again.

At first, it was just about trying the products. Your hair started to look and feel better—shinier, healthier, more like the version of you that you remembered. Your confidence grew a little, too.

Then came the next step: you showed up on Instagram stories talking to what felt like yourself half the time. Then you did your first Instagram Live. Your hands were shaking, your voice a little unsure—but you did it anyway. And something happened. People responded. They connected. Not all at once, but slowly and surely.

That moment cracked something open in you. The idea that maybe you didn't have to be perfectly polished or professional to be impactful. You just had to be real.

Later came your first time speaking publicly. Your heart was pounding. You had to breathe through the nerves. But you stood in front of a room full of women, vulnerable and imperfect, and you shared your story. And they leaned in. Because it wasn't about having all the answers—it was about showing what was possible when you start taking small, brave steps.

Then came your first team training. You led a group. You mentored. You taught. And with every call, every voice memo, every pep talk you gave, your belief in yourself got stronger. Your voice steadier. Your purpose clearer.

Through it all, this business didn't just bring you an income—it brought you a transformation. You were learning so many new things. To lead. To market. To serve. To believe in yourself in ways you didn't even know you needed. That's when you realized: this wasn't just about beauty products. It was about becoming.

You found yourself again, but in a new and improved way—but you weren't quite done yet.

Even with all of this growth, you still didn't always love how you looked in photos. You were still unsure of how to dress your evolving self. You had your confidence back, but your reflection didn't always feel in sync with it.

And then you discovered color analysis.

You were sitting at a beauty convention in 2023 when some of your teammates pulled up TikTok reels about it. At first, it felt like just another trend. But something deeper tugged at you. Because while your style had always felt deeply personal, maybe even niche, color felt universal. Color didn't care about body type, budget, or trends. Color was for everyone.

And it felt like the next step in your evolution. The bridge between your love for style, your passion for wellness, and your growing mission to help women feel like themselves again.

And that was the day your next chapter began.

At the time, no one in your area was offering seasonal color analysis in a modern, relatable, and accessible way. So you decided to be that person. You trained, studied, and integrated color theory into your existing beauty brand, because it made sense. Color was the missing piece in the healthy aging conversation. Women were already investing in skincare, haircare, wellness, but many were still lost on how to dress, how to express, how to feel at home in their own skin again.

When you discovered you were a True Winter, everything clicked. You saw yourself in bold jewel tones—cool magentas, rich sapphires, deep emeralds—and something inside you shifted.

You sat in front of the mirror and saw your face transform. No makeup, no filters, no tricks. Just fabric and light. And for the first time in years, your reflection felt honest.

You looked more energized. More vibrant. More you. Not the you that had to work for beauty, but the you that had it all along—it was just waiting to be framed by the right tones.

You started showing up online without filters for the first time in. You edited your photos less. You started getting compliments from your husband, friends, and strangers, along with comments on your content saying, "You're glowing." But the truth is, the glow wasn't just your skin—it was your alignment.

You realized: this wasn't just a tool. This was a revolution. And you wanted to bring it home.

And that's the key. You weren't trying to change anyone. You were helping them see themselves again.

Now, you drape women from all walks of life: new moms rediscovering their confidence, women going through divorce, women healing from loss, professionals reentering the workforce, or creatives trying to show up on camera without second-guessing everything. Each one of them comes in with a story. And each one of them leaves with a mirror that tells the truth.

Because the wrong colors don't just wash us out—they tell a false narrative. They create dark shadows under our eyes. They make our skin look uneven. They age us unnecessarily. And worse, they reinforce the quiet lie that we're somehow "not enough."

But the right colors?

They restore us.

They energize our skin.

They lift our features.

They make us look younger—yes—but more importantly, they help us feel whole.

You've now had the privilege of watching hundreds of women glow up in your chair—not because of vanity, but because they see themselves clearly for the first time in a long time.

This work has been your joy and your calling. You've partnered with businesses. You've hosted masterclass events. You've used your voice to help women connect with their reflection in the most life-giving way. You've been invited into their stories, and they've become part of yours.

Looking back, you're proud of the way you followed the breadcrumbs. From leaving corporate life to chasing confidence. From filtering photos to filtering out the noise. From simply needing to recreate your own income to building impact. From trembling in your first Instagram Live to mentoring others to find their own voice.

You never could've predicted that a filtered vacation photo would lead to a chapter like this, but here you are.

Color brought you home to yourself.

And now, you're holding the door open for everyone else.

With love (and magenta lipstick),
You

About Anoushka

Anoushka Dannin is a respected seasonal color analyst and content creator with a background in finance turned entrepreneur. With a passion for helping women embrace their natural beauty and personal style, Anoushka has built a powerful platform focused on confidence, color, and clean beauty.

She began her journey as a financial analyst, and later found her calling in the beauty and wellness industry, using social media to inspire a healthy, confident approach to aging and self-expression.

She built a thriving business in the clean beauty industry, where she was in the top five percent in a global beauty company, earning multiple incentive trips, a car allowance, mentoring hundreds of women and speaking at corporate events to share her entrepreneurial journey.

Her influence has earned her recognition as one of the Top 30 Las Vegas Influencers by *Entrepreneurs Magazine* in 2020 and in *89052 Magazine* and *South Vegas City Lifestyle Magazine*. She has also been a guest on Channel 8's lifestyle show *Las Vegas TV Now* and a speaker at KBIS, where she spoke about the impact of color in personal branding.

With a combined following of over 300,000 on TikTok and Instagram, Anoushka uses her platform to mentor women and amplify messages around confidence, personal branding, and style. She is also a dedicated community volunteer, actively giving back to numerous organizations, most recently via the Young Men's Service League alongside her son.

Instagram and TikTok: @ForYourReputation
https://www.foryourreputation.com/

Alchemical Disruption

Jessica Jay Dee

Nothing I do—or have ever done—makes sense. Not really. My resume reads like it has ADHD, and my experience zigzags across industries and ideologies with no regard for societal norms or traditions. I didn't follow the rules. I never have. But every deviation taught me something vital: success isn't linear, and rules were made to be rewritten. The lesson? You don't need permission to live a meaningful life—just purpose.

I was born in Champaign, Ill., raised on fried catfish, skinned knees, and country music. Cornfields and cow pastures were my backdrop, and Randy Travis and George Strait wrote the soundtrack to my childhood. We moved to Colorado Springs when I was young, but the country never quite left me. I still carry the soil of that upbringing under my nails. From humble beginnings, I learned that roots matter—but wings matter more. Build your launch pad from your past, not your prison.

At seventeen years old, before the world changed on September 11th, I joined the United States Marine Corps. Why? At the time, I thought I had something to prove—maybe to my family, maybe to the world. But now I know I had something to prove to myself. The truth is, no external validation can fill the void of untapped potential. The lesson? You are the permission slip you've been waiting for.

I come from a long line of warriors. Not all fought wars in uniform, but their battles were no less noble. My mother's lineage traces back to Navajo, Ute, and Tewa ancestors, perhaps as far as the Spanish-American War. Her fight wasn't overseas, though. It was right at home, beside my father, whose battle with alcoholism was catalyzed by a car accident. When he stumbled, she picked up the sword. From them, I learned that warriors wear many faces, and strength is sometimes soft and silent. Love can be the fiercest armor of all.

Mom began as a housekeeper at La Quinta Inn, graduated to managing private homes, and then, against all odds, became the housekeeping manager at the five-star, five-diamond Broadmoor Hotel. In her forties, she earned her GED, then her associate's degree, and eventually followed her calling to work with special needs children. Through it all, she remained a steadfast wife and believer. She and my father were married forty-four years before he passed in 2018, not long after a painful relapse. Her resilience reminded me that faith isn't perfection—it's perseverance. Legacy isn't built in loud wins; it's built in quiet consistency.

As a young high school graduate, still green and on my own for the first time, Marine Corps boot camp didn't break me—I had already been forged by life. Four years of Junior ROTC had prepped me with discipline and military customs. Women recruits trained at Parris Island, S.C. Our mornings began at four a.m., lights out at eight p.m. We did what we were told. We ran. We cleaned. We endured. I learned to find purpose in repetition, and power in surrendering to the process. Show up, even when no one's clapping.

During the second month, I found myself punished again on the quarterdeck. Burpees, pushups, flutter kicks—a blur of movement and sweat. But something changed. I realized I could outlast them. The punishment became a privilege. Pain became power. That was the moment I transformed. Discomfort became my teacher. Resilience became my reward. Lesson? If you can survive discomfort, you can achieve anything.

Then came the Crucible—a fifty-four-hour test of endurance and resolve. With little food, less sleep, and one mission: survive together. Bonds formed through suffering taught me that shared struggle creates unshakable trust. We earned our Eagle, Globe, and Anchor. The Warrior Breakfast that followed was more than food—it was a sacred transformation. I learned that the most nourishing moments come after the most exhausting climbs. Lesson? You are forged, not found.

I served as an air traffic controller and was named Controller of the Year as a corporal. I became a top trainer at one of the busiest stations in the Corps. Later, I taught at the Navy and Marine Corps ATC School. Watching students connect the dots gave me life. Mastery, I learned, isn't about what you know—it's about how well you can translate that power into others. Share your genius. It's the only way it grows.

In Iraq, I made decisions that changed the trajectory of lives. I didn't pull triggers, but I launched the aircraft that did. That reckoning shaped me. I served with pride and prayer and still carry the echoes of those calls. Honor, I discovered, isn't black and white. It's grey, heavy, and often asks more questions than it answers. Still, I showed up. Lesson? Do the best you can with what you have—and ask for forgiveness when the silence falls.

Later, as group legal chief, I mastered the Uniform Code of Military Justice and earned the Navy Commendation Medal. I thought about law. Then came embassy duty—leading Marine detachments in Haiti, Prague, and Havana. I protected secrets, managed crises, and coordinated diplomacy. I fell in love with precision, ceremony, and elevated execution. In high-stakes environments, I learned that composure is currency.

I was selected for the female infantry trial but declined, despite qualifying. I didn't believe in the policy and wouldn't be its face. My Marines respected me more for that decision. I had already proven everything I needed to prove. Lesson? Integrity means walking away from the spotlight when it blinds your truth.

I left the Corps at thirty. I had eight years left until retirement, but I didn't need a pension to validate my worth. I needed a new mountain to climb. I was ready to build something of my own.

Pro Chic Events was born. My first wedding included three dress changes and ten plated courses. My last, on Catalina Island, was a $1.5 million orchestration. Chaos never tasted so sweet. Winning People's Choice at Denver International Live Events Association was a nod from the universe: you're still in the arena. The lesson? Grace under fire isn't optional. It's the job.

Betrayal came. A protégé stole my playbook and launched a competing brand. I took legal action, healed, and recalibrated. Lesson? Trust, but leave a paper trail. And always keep your crown straight, even when it's shaking.

Next came coaching and consulting. Entrepreneurs came to me with dreams; I gave them blueprints. Clarity. Courage. Brand identity. Operational systems. Emotional agility. They left transformed. The lesson? Give away your wisdom. Keep the magic flowing.

In 2017, I re-read *The Alchemist*. Meditated. Failed. Wrote anyway. *The Alchemy Effect*™ was born—not as a brand, but a vibration. A heartbeat. A homecoming. It is my soul's work. The lesson? Stop waiting for clarity. Begin, and clarity will find you.

Spirituality found me. Not in churches, but in whispers, visions, and truths I couldn't ignore. Raised Catholic, trained as a skeptic, I now know that divinity dances in synchronicities. The manuscript holds those moments. They aren't polished. But they are sacred. The lesson? You are more than flesh. You are frequency.

I am a survivor of military sexual trauma. I didn't report. I wasn't ready. Silence protected me then. Words free me now. I hold space for all who walk this line. The lesson? Your healing is yours. Name it when you're ready. Or not at all.

Since then, I've worn a hundred hats. Security advisor. Martial arts instructor. Hollywood consultant. Retail manager. Producer. Strategist. Dreamer. I passed polygraphs and background checks most people couldn't imagine. I've failed, risen, wept, and celebrated. The lesson? Titles mean little. Character means everything.

Today, I live in Las Vegas. I coach. I create. I disrupt. I work strictly off referrals and only say yes to aligned collaborations. Many of my clients—from celebrity names to stealth-mode startups—require non-disclosure agreements, which adds a certain allure. But let me be clear: behind the velvet ropes and curated perfection, the lives of the rich and famous are not always glamorous. Money doesn't buy happiness. It buys complexity. It buys mirrors that show you who people really are when they're winning.

Operating in that rarefied space, I have become a silent advisor. Trusted. Strategic. Invisible in plain sight. I gain access others can't, connect dots no one else sees, and make magic behind the curtain—not for fame, but for fulfillment. I've held many titles and worn many hats, but today I enjoy the privilege of choosing who I partner with. That freedom? It is the most luxurious currency I know.

The Alchemy Effect™ is a spiritual fine jewelry line, a forthcoming (long-awaited) manuscript, a podcast, a mastermind, and a lifestyle collective and community. Not a brand—a way of being. A return to authentic self. A fearlessness. A reminder that your pain can be precious. I cannot wait to share more of this labor of love with you.

If you're still reading, thank you. You now know me. My story is not unique because of what I've done, but because I refuse to stop becoming. I don't know what I want to be when I grow up—but I've had a hell of a start figuring it out.

So, here's my advice:

- Continuously redefine your treasure.
- Leave every room better than you found it.
- Brighten someone's path, especially when they can't see their own.
- Trust your intuition, especially when it's inconvenient or uncomfortable.
- Keep your word. Especially to yourself.
- Love. Fully. Even if it breaks you.
- Trust. But verify.
- Stay soft. This world needs your velvet fire.

And above all—be your own alchemist.
Disrupt. Transform. Begin again.

About Jessica

Jessica Jay Dee is a highly decorated United States Marine Corps veteran, now operating as a discreet and in-demand strategic consultant for founders, creators, and high-growth businesses across multiple industries. With experience overseeing operating environments exceeding half a billion dollars and directing multimillion-dollar events, she brings a rare combination of battlefield-tested leadership, intuitive brand vision, and practical execution to everything she builds.

Jessica advises an exclusive roster of clients—many under NDA—including celebrities, stealth-mode startups, and enterprise-level organizations. Her work is high-impact, high-integrity, and entirely referral-based. She is a silent advisor who thrives behind the scenes, connecting dots others miss and transforming complexity into clarity and legacy.

As the founder of *The Alchemy Effect*™, Jessica curates a growing suite of offerings, including a spiritual fine jewelry line, a soon-to-be-released manuscript, a podcast, mastermind experiences, and immersive lifestyle activations. More than a brand, *The Alchemy Effect* is a way of being—founded on disruption, transformation, and the courage to leave the ordinary behind.

www.jessicajaydee.com
Instagram: @jessica.jay.dee
www.thealchemyeffect.com
Instagram: @thealchemyeffect

From Chaos to Calm: Designing a Life with Purpose

Lucille Dela Rosa

I didn't always dream of becoming an entrepreneur. Like many people, I followed the path I thought I was supposed to take—earn a degree, land a corporate job, and climb the ladder. And for a while, I did just that.

Growing up in a traditional Filipino household, my parents always stressed the importance of academics. Get good grades. Earn a college degree. Secure a high-paying job. I was a shy, reserved child—the quiet one in class who kept to herself and felt overwhelmed by the pressure to perform. I struggled in school, especially with subjects like math, and while many of my peers were high achievers receiving scholarships and university acceptances, I was attending community college, unsure of what I truly wanted.

But I always had art. Drawing came naturally to me. I went from sketching cartoon characters to designing houses and floor plans. One day, a family member looked at my sketches and said, "These are very nice! You should get into architecture." I remember everyone nodding in agreement, excited by the idea of a stable, respected career path. But inside, I was paralyzed with fear. I was already struggling academically—how could I ever make it as an architect?

Still, I tried. I pursued architecture classes, all while working retail at the local mall. But the more I forced it, the more disconnected I felt. Eventually, I pivoted to interior design and transferred to The Art Institute of Las Vegas. There, I felt something click. I was still scared and uncertain, but I finally felt like I was on a path that aligned with my talents.

After graduating, I entered the world of hospitality interior design—working on luxury hotels, casinos, and timeshares across the United States, Mexico, the Caribbean, and Canada. It felt like a dream job at first. I was designing for spaces that thousands of people would walk through every day. But the fast-paced, high-pressure corporate world quickly took its toll. I was overworked, underpaid, and emotionally drained.

I endured long days, condescending coworkers, and moments where I held back tears in my cubicle. Even when I switched jobs, hoping for a better culture, I still felt like an underdog. Despite holding a degree and having years of experience, I constantly questioned if I was good enough or smart enough to belong.

Then came the pandemic. I was let go from my position. Just like that, everything I had worked for vanished. I found myself in a deep depressive state, stuck at home, unsure of my next move. My health deteriorated. I was in and out of doctors' offices, battling fatigue and infections no one could explain. One doctor finally said, "Maybe it's environmental."

That comment shifted everything. I looked around my home—really looked. It wasn't peaceful. It wasn't functional. It certainly wasn't a healing space. I began to wonder if my environment was contributing to my declining health—and that of my kids, who struggled with asthma and allergies.

So I started making changes. I created a self-care corner in my bedroom. I swapped out synthetic materials for natural ones, brought in plants, rearranged furniture to create better flow, and removed unnecessary clutter. I focused less on aesthetics and more on function and feeling. Slowly, my mental health began to improve. My physical health followed. My relationships healed, including a friendship I had impulsively ended in the darkest days of my depression.

It became clear: if I could heal through intentional design, others could too.

That's when Lucy Dee Interiors was born. I launched my wellness-centered interior design studio during the pandemic, starting with virtual services and small design packages on Etsy. At first, I was just trying to stay afloat. But over time, it grew. I attracted clients who weren't just looking for pretty spaces—they were searching for peace.

One of my first projects was a large Airbnb renovation, and at the time, it felt like a dream. I loved being involved in construction and seeing transformations come to life. But over the years, I realized that the big, high-end projects didn't actually align with who I was. I wasn't interested in chasing luxury or trends. I wanted to help people who were going through similar challenges that I faced.

As a solo designer, I found joy in smaller, more manageable projects. Projects that allowed me to be fully present, creative, and intentional. I stopped trying to blend in with what everyone else was doing in the design world. I stopped chasing what looked successful and instead focused on what felt purposeful.

Being a mom has shaped everything I do. My children are my why. Their struggles with allergies and asthma reminded me of the importance of designing for wellness. My own mental health journey taught me that a home should nurture you. That's why I don't just design for aesthetics. I design for health, harmony, and healing.

My process is deeply personal. I take the time to understand how my clients want to feel in their homes. Then we co-create spaces that reflect those feelings. Whether it's a calming reading nook, a functional kitchen, or a full home refresh, the goal is always the same: to help people feel supported, seen, and at peace.

Today, Lucy Dee Interiors serves busy professionals, families, and individuals who crave more than just a beautiful home. They want a space that helps them feel grounded, inspired, and whole. I've helped parents create routines, guided families through renovations, and designed intentional homes for people navigating grief, change, and healing.

Entrepreneurship isn't easy. There are seasons of doubt, slow months, and moments where I wonder if I'm doing enough. But every client who tells me, "This changed everything," reminds me why I started.

Now, I'm expanding Lucy Dee Interiors to include digital design kits, passive income products, and educational tools to empower others to design with purpose—even if they're doing it themselves. My hope is that everyone can experience the transformation that comes from living in a space that truly supports them.

When I think about what it means to "slay," I think of women like me. Women who overcame adversity. Who turned pain into purpose. Who chose authenticity over acceptance.

I didn't build Lucy Dee Interiors to impress. I built it to make an impact. To create spaces where people can heal, grow, and feel at home.

And that, to me, is everything.

About Lucille

Lucille Dela Rosa is the founder of Lucy Dee Interiors, a Las Vegas-based interior design studio rooted in wellness, functionality, and intention. With a background in hospitality design, Lucille began her career designing luxury spaces for hotels, casinos, and timeshares across the United States, Mexico, the Caribbean, and Canada after earning her bachelor's degree from The Art Institute of Las Vegas.

But in 2020, everything changed. After being laid off during the pandemic, Lucille found herself not only without a job, but also struggling with mysterious health issues and a depleted sense of purpose. The culprit, she realized, may have been closer than she thought—her own environment.

That realization sparked a powerful mission: to create interiors that not only look beautiful but also support the health and well-being of the people living in them. Today, Lucy Dee Interiors specializes in purposeful design that puts people first. Through a holistic lens, Lucille helps clients transform their homes into restorative, functional spaces that nourish the mind, body, and soul.

Whether working virtually with families nationwide or designing in-person for clients across Las Vegas, Lucille is deeply committed to improving lives—one intentional space at a time.

lucydeeinteriors.com
Instagram: @lucydeeinteriors

Faith Through Fire

Kandice Delgado

If you told me this is how my life would have turned out, I would have never believed you. If you told me as a little girl that one day I'd be a successful, self-employed, internationally sought-after makeup artist, flown across the world, working with celebrities, and mentoring others, I would've never believed you. Not because I didn't want to, but because where I came from, no one ever taught me it was okay to dream like that. I'm not sure there was room for me to dream at all.

We rehearse our story in our minds so often that by the time we are asked to tell it, we shrink it down. We lead with bullet points, accolades, or job titles. But I don't want to do that here. I want to show you that there's a dream life *beyond* your trauma, hope after loss, abundance beyond scarcity, success after hardships, and love after heartbreak. The very things you feel have held you back most in life, scarred you, and jolted you, are meant to be the very platform you stand on to help others. Your story was never meant to break you; it was meant to shape you and be the very fire that lights the path in front of you and others.

I didn't grow up hearing, "You can be anything." I didn't have parents preparing me for college or teaching me how to lead a beautiful, fulfilling life. I was put up for adoption at birth, and raised by my grandmother, my saving grace. My mother was emotionally unavailable. My father only met me a handful of times before telling me he was starting a new family and that I would never see him again.

At fifteen, I found myself completely on my own. No safety net. No back-up plan. Just my will to create a life for myself greater than the one I was born into, and a fire in my spirit whispering, *you were made for more.*

Even though I was put up for adoption, I wasn't without love. God, in His mercy, surrounded me with glimpses of what family could look like, even if it wasn't always traditional. People who, in their own quiet ways, taught me to dream simply by how they loved. My uncle would mentor his daughters so beautifully, and he always made sure there was a seat for me at the table. My aunt loved her children so deeply and folded me into that love. My cousins became my constant, holding me together through every mountain and valley. Their love filled me with exactly what I needed...*hope.*

It taught me that love doesn't need to be perfect to be powerful. That life is all about perspective. That sometimes, God sends you family through the people who stay, who see you, and fight for you in the ways they know how. I learned to seek out the glimmers—when you pay attention, you realize they are everywhere.

I became a preschool teacher not because that was my dream, but because that seemed like the most stable and practical thing to do. It seemed safe. But it wasn't until I stood in a MAC Cosmetics store watching my cousin apply makeup on someone that I felt a shift. The artists were stylish, confident, and magnetic, and I wanted to be one of them. I didn't know you could make a living doing makeup. I didn't know if someone like me could afford that risk, but something in me said: *What if?*

See, my uncle also taught me one of the most valuable lessons I would ever learn in my life: the power of manifestation. He taught me to go after my dreams even if they feel terrifying. The saying, "If your dreams don't scare you, they are not big enough," has been used by some of the most prolific people across history.

I was terrified, but I had become good at doing hard things. So I started as a six-hour artist at one of the lowest-traffic malls in the valley. Within a few short years, I was managing one of the top ten MAC locations in the country. From there, the door kept opening. I became a specialty artist in artist relations. I worked on the iconic Mariah Carey residency in Las Vegas. Clients followed me from location to location. Eventually, the demand outside of MAC grew so consistently that I was faced with a decision: stay in the safety of the most reliable job I'd known up to that point, or take a leap and go completely independent, something very few artists did successfully at the time.

I decided to take a leap of faith. I went on to work with global brands like Pretty Little Thing, Fashion Nova, Oh Polly, and Naked Wardrobe. I worked with Gabrielle Union, recording artist Cassie, and countless others. Brides flew across the world to work with me, and I was flown across the world to work with them. And even now, every time it happens, I am still in awe.

I wasn't the most qualified. I didn't have formal training or years of education. There were times I felt unqualified. *But God does not call the qualified; He qualifies the called.*

None of this happened by accident; it wasn't hustle, luck, or done in my own strength. I did it with God.

I've always had faith. As a little girl, I spoke to God like He was my father—because honestly, He was. When I was a child, I prayed to survive. Then I prayed to dream. I prayed for the doors to open. And every time I prayed specifically, God answered specifically.

The truth is trauma doesn't just shape us, it will try to narrate our story. And healing is about reclaiming the pen.

I used to think that healing looked like forgetting or being able to tell your story without crying. But now I know healing looks like remembering, so you can reclaim it. So you can become everything your younger self was quietly hoping you'd grow into.

Healing for me has looked like therapy, journaling, reading the Word, crying on the floor, getting up again, taking care of my body for the first time, hearing God after silence, and saying yes to myself even when I was scared. Healing looked like no longer being defined by survival mode but becoming the woman God called me to be.

It also looked like building something bigger than myself. I co-founded the Make-up Your Mindset Community with two of my cousins, both artists, visionaries, survivors. Together, we coach beauty entrepreneurs not just on building a business, but building a life rooted in purpose. We teach a mindset that reshapes identity. We teach vision that creates alignment. We teach belief that refuses to quit.

I learned that your trauma doesn't disqualify you. It equips you. I know what it's like to lose a parent. I know what it's like to walk through a divorce. I know what it's like to experience depression and still get up the next day to try again.

I've learned that you can be brokenhearted and still be blessed. You can be healing and still be chosen. I know what it's like to walk through fire. Because I lived it.

Nineteen years after I had last seen my biological father, he called and asked to meet as if no time had passed, unaware that it was my thirty-fourth birthday. I sat across from him at a small café. I thought maybe it would bring answers, closure or at least help the missing pieces settle into place. But instead, God gave me something far more powerful. He gave me clarity. In the stillness of that moment, I heard Him speak in a way I had never experienced before. He said, "Do you see now what I was doing, protecting you from? You were never like them; you were like me."

Psalms 27:10 says, "If your own mother and father abandon you, I myself, the Lord, will take you in." And He did. Not just once, but over and over again. In every season where I felt overlooked, He was covering me. Every moment I questioned why I had to walk alone, He was walking beside me. I just didn't know it yet.

That day, something in me shifted. It was like God reached into the deepest part of my story and rewrote it with truth. I stopped chasing love that had already been given to me. I stopped trying to prove I was worthy of what God had already called good. I stopped quieting the light He placed inside me just to make others more comfortable in their own darkness.

I was never the unwanted daughter of flawed people. I was the chosen daughter of a perfect Father. I was never abandoned. I was protected. I was never disqualified. I was being forged in fire.

I believe our stories are never meant to end in trauma, but begin in triumph. I believe everything we go through is preparation. That rejection is redirection. That abandonment can be protection. You don't need to be perfect. You don't need to come from a picture-perfect family. You need purpose. You need faith. You need people who speak life into the places where lies once lived. And most importantly, you need to remember the same God who created the stars created you, and He does not make mistakes.

If you are reading this and you feel stuck, like your story disqualifies you, I want to remind you that your trauma does not define you. It builds you. Remember Ephesians 3:20, "Now to him who is able to do immeasurably more than all we ask or imagine, according to his power that is at work within us." The rejection, the heartbreak, the waiting, the silence, the hard work and the tears when no one is watching are not the end; they are the training ground for your testimony.

So, whether you are a makeup artist, a writer, an entrepreneur, or a woman picking herself up again, I want you to know that if God did it for me, He will do it for you, too.

About Kandice

Kandice Delgado is an international makeup artist and faith-based entrepreneur whose story is rooted in resilience, vision, and unwavering belief. Raised in an unconventional environment without financial or emotional support, Kandice knows firsthand what it means to build from the ground up with nothing but faith, grit, and a dream.

She began her career as a preschool teacher, choosing the most practical path, but later followed her heart into makeup artistry. That decision changed everything. What started as a dream became a global career. Kandice has worked on high-profile campaigns for PrettyLittleThing, Fashion Nova, Oh Polly, and Naked Wardrobe. Her work has been featured in *People* and *Bride* magazines, and she has had the honor of working with Gabrielle Union, recording artist Cassie, and during the legendary Mariah Carey residency in Las Vegas.

Kandice is living proof that you can come from anywhere and still achieve your wildest dreams.

Today, she is also a writer, speaker, and co-founder of Makeup Your Mindset, a community that empowers beauty entrepreneurs to scale their businesses and step into their God-given purpose. With deep compassion and a heart committed to service, Kandice continues to pour into those around her, reminding them that with faith, anything is possible.

Instagram: @kandicedelgado
Tiktok: @kandicedelgado

The Quiet Architect: Between the Lines and the Lights

Melissa "Dot" Desrameaux

I remember the first time I held *Anthologically Speaking*, my coffee table book, printed and bound. A concept that whispered from my heart for years finally had weight in my hands. The glossy cover encased over one hundred sixty pages crisp enough to deserve a finger lick. It was more than publishing. It felt like I designed a space, much like I've done for years in events, but this time with language. That moment is better described as a homecoming rather than a launch; a long-held truth finding its voice.

That same moment reminded me of my younger self who scribbled verses in the margins of notebooks, unsure if the words would ever matter to anyone but me. I found myself rereading a poem I wrote at twenty-two while trying to make sense of what it meant to be visible, to be whole, to be heard.

My anthology is filled with visual art and poems that were written over the course of two decades. Some were pulled from journals kept when I was fifteen. Others arrived in the haze of adulthood, when I was elbows-deep in building budgets, event briefs, production runs, and drafting newsletters. My constant has always been this: a desire to understand people and create spaces, literal or lyrical, where they could feel something real.

Las Vegas is always alive beyond the panes of my downtown high-rise's windows. Flickering lights, the whirl of helicopters, pulsing music, and sirens fold into the fabric of the night. As frequently as I enjoy slipping into the buzz to observe or adventure, I understand that the best experiences are rarely about the creator but about what's been created. I've spent years building environments and designing moments that wrap people in color, sound, scent, and surprise. In the stillness between experiences, I think of words and how they stretch time, lingering longer than confetti. I believe that magic lives in the moments that do not receive applause. I stand in awe of rooms that can breathe because they were designed to hold both emotion and motion. My work exists in that in-between, the crossroads of narrative and experience.

It started with words and a love of storytelling within an immigrant family where silence said more than language ever could. As a kid, I was always watching people, studying gestures and mapping tone to subtext. I learned to listen for what wasn't said. That instinct started earlier than I realized. Maybe that's what happens when you grow up between cultures. Your eyes become fluent before your voice does. Being raised in a Haitian household while moving through American spaces made me a lifelong translator: of meaning, of intention, of mood. That early sensitivity became the foundation of my professional ethos. I studied mass communications at Florida International University thinking I'd go into journalism or PR, but what I really wanted was to help shape how people feel when they encounter something: a brand, a room, a message, each a kind of poem if you tilt your head the right way. And now, that same watchfulness serves me in ways I could never have predicted. It helps me anticipate client needs before they're spoken. It gives me the ability to thread a brand's story across mediums through mood boards and messaging, spatial design and sound. I've come to understand that a good strategy not only answers a question, but it listens for the question underneath.

That's the thread, I think. The one that connects the girl writing poems under a desk lamp in the suburbs of Miramar, Fla., to the woman operating an event space off-strip in Las Vegas. The girl who questioned if she was enough to the woman who now curates rooms filled with energy, electricity, and belonging. My work may be production-forward, tech-enabled, and experiential, but it's always been about story. I produce events while making space for the people inside those events to feel seen. That's been an underlying mission for quite some time. Whether I'm leading a meeting, putting together a creative pitch, or designing a multi-sensory activation, my best work requires presence, not only polish. What I've built is rarely just visual. It's spatial storytelling. The invitation, the lighting, the pacing, the way a guest moves through the experience. Every detail is a verse. I design events with the same intention I give to a line of poetry. A beat here. A light cue there. A shift in color or focus to nudge the energy from curiosity to connection. I don't think of myself as an event producer as much as an architect of feeling and flow. The most common medium happens to be physical space and human presence.

Earlier this year, I hosted a salon-style launch for *Anthologically Speaking* in downtown Las Vegas. Yes, it was about the book, but it was also about creating a space where people could exhale, reflect, and witness each other beyond the surface. We had soft jazz in the background, cozy lounges, and visual art projected and looping on the wall. Some guests came in business attire. Others showed up in jeans with sneakers and wide eyes. But everyone showed up curious, and that was enough. At one point in the night, I stood beneath the soft wash of teal lighting, holding my book loosely. I wasn't performing. I was offering. I watched someone dog-ear a page in the book, and another person silently smirk at a line I was once too afraid to share, as I gave a talk about unspoken truths weaving in seven poems that speak on being social and open in vulnerable spaces.

That's the kind of energy I try to bring into my work, even in a city that's known for overstimulation. Las Vegas thrives on spectacle, but what I crave and what I think people are starting to crave more of is sensation with depth. Spaces that invite presence alongside performance. My work at StarBase is positioned for strategy, creativity, and community. It's a versatile venue powered by Fresh Wata, an event design and production company with teams that transform a blank room into a cinematic landscape or a tactile playground. We've hosted everything from immersive auto shows, product launches, and custom brand activations with full-scale digital integration to high school proms, comedy shows, and symposiums. What most people don't see is the invisible thread beneath it all: empathy. Before an event, I walk through the space like I'm walking through someone's memory in advance. I imagine where their eyes will land, where they'll pause, where they'll feel held. I consider what they might need to feel comfortable enough to engage. Those aren't simply details. They're the design.

And yet, for a long time, I didn't know if there was room for someone like me to lead in these spaces. I don't come from a family of artists or executives. I come from Haitian lineage. First-gen grit. Hospitality, yes, but also humility. Getting here wasn't effortless. I learned to lead by listening. I learned to speak by writing when it was too intimidating to take up room aloud. It wasn't until I stepped fully into myself that I shifted my perspective from the discomfort of being flawed to being a bridge. It took time to trust that being the quiet one in the room didn't mean being the least impactful.

My restraint was its own kind of power. I used to dim myself in spaces where I didn't see reflections of my own story—where race, gender, or lack of familiarity with the room's community made me feel peripheral. Somewhere along the way, I stopped asking for permission. I started leading with intention. Now, I'm invited to speak at conferences like NAB, where I share insights on hybrid event design and the evolving role of AI, or join podcasts to explore the emotional layers behind creative work with stories, lessons, and the feelings we often leave unspoken. I continue to lead a standout creative venue, build collaborative teams, and advise on campaigns designed to resonate beyond a single moment. But I still write poems in the quiet between the storms. And I still believe in the power of softness, not as weakness, but as a form of precision, clarity, and direction.

I don't think I'll ever stop toggling between the poetic and the pragmatic. I don't wish to. This is who I am: an artist in an architect's suit. A builder of atmosphere and intimacy. A woman in Las Vegas who sees the glitter, and chooses to add glow. The poems in my book aren't polished to perfection. Some are tender. Others are uncertain. But together, they map the quiet evolution of a girl who once wrote under her breath and now builds spaces that speak louder than words. Whether it's a poem, a light cue, or a perfectly timed pause, I'm always designing for feeling, for arrival. That's where you'll find me: not in the spotlight, but in the stillness underneath it, shaping stories in space. One moment, one metaphor, one room at a time.

About Melissa

Melissa "Dot" Desrameaux is a weaver of worlds where sound meets soul, and spaces become stories. A native of South Florida now rooted in Las Vegas, she brings over a decade of creative instinct and strategic fire to the art of experience. As venue director at StarBase, an event venue owned and operated by Fresh Wata, Melissa curates immersive, sensory-rich environments that both entertain and awaken.

A creative architect of connection and culture, she blends her expertise and taste across event design, production, communications, and hospitality to craft spaces that spark interaction, conversation, and meaningful connection. Her journey includes shaping campaigns and environments with standout teams. Whether producing a pop-up, launching a brand, or reimagining a venue, she brings bold vision and soulful strategy to every pursuit.

Melissa is a proud graduate of Florida International University with a degree in mass communications, concentrating in public relations. She leads with energy, empathy, and a flair for the immersive, creating moments that invite people to pause, reflect, reconnect with themselves and one another. She is also a poet and author, recently self-publishing her first anthology—part art book, part love letter to becoming. Styled as a coffee table companion, her writing explores identity, resilience, intimacy, and imagination with raw grace. Her words echo the same intentionality she brings to her events: creating not just what's seen, but what's deeply felt.

www.starbaselv.com
Instagram: @starbaselv

Focus on the Good

Mackenna Dugan

I'll never forget the moment it all changed for me. I wish I could say it was some spectacular sign from the universe that gave me goosebumps and the courage to start over. Rather, it was any other day at the gym, at a squat rack, where my eyes caught my reflection in the mirror and I saw myself for the first time. I dropped down into my set, broken and lost, a victim to the world and all the circumstances that led me there. But I rose up from that very same set changed. It was like the veil had been lifted, and I wasn't settling for this pathetic existence I designed anymore.

I had every valid reason in the book to feel victimized by life. Traumatic childhood, rebellious teenager who never quite fit in, a long list of toxic relationships, and zero passions or interests other than shit talking with my friends. But there was always a whisper, and that day it was roaring...YOU ARE MEANT FOR MORE. I chose to believe it.

What began after this moment was years of self-discovery. Things got harder before there was ever a light at the end of the tunnel. I worked through conditioned belief systems and generational trauma; I learned to disassociate from my thoughts and consciously choose new ones that resonated. I read books, tried meditation, started a journaling practice, surrounded myself with conscious people, including my now husband Jonathon, and engaged in conversations that were far outside my comfort zone. I fell in love with myself and eventually felt worthy of a life of purpose, passion and joy. *Disclaimer: I was worthy the whole time, it just took me a minute to realize it.*

But how do you pursue something you love when you don't know what you love? I felt this one deeply to my core. You might know all these people who have been passionately pursuing a goal for their entire lives, and you're like, "must be nice to know who you are and what you want." Ya, me too.

Even with all this newfound wisdom about chasing a life I loved, I didn't even know what I freaking loved! So what did I do? I started to try on some personalities. This one felt too tight, that one made me anxious, and that weird one over there was sort of cute, but I couldn't see myself wearing it every day.

And that's when I found yoga.

You might be thinking, *but Mackenna, aren't you a photographer?* Yeah, well I never said the first thing you go all in on is gonna be your thing. The point I'm trying to make is that you have to start somewhere. You're never gonna know until you try—a cliché, I know... but there's something to it.

Yoga was foundational for me. I continued to dive deep into myself, and the mindset and physical practices were transformational. But it still didn't light me up, particularly when I tried to make a living from it. So I put my aspirations on pause as my boyfriend Jonathon and I found out we were pregnant with a baby boy.

My journey from maiden to mother is one to be explored another time. We welcomed Emerson Forest after an attempted home birth, a traumatic transfer to the hospital, and a vaginal breech delivery that defied all the odds. Maybe we'll revisit my journey in my next book; for now, let's fast forward to my postpartum journey after his birth.

I had always known I wanted to be a mom. It was the one thing I was sure about. My boyfriend had a son, Greyson Wilder, and I was intimately involved in his life right after he turned one. My relationship with him confirmed for me that being a mother was an absolute must.

So here I am, with a five-month-old, in the throes of postpartum depression and not knowing what's next for me. I was feeling insanely guilty that "just" being a mom was not enough, and an idea popped into my head: *You should go buy that professional camera you've always wanted.*

Let's be clear. Yes, photography was always something I loved; as my father's old home videos can confirm, I love to be in front of the camera and behind it. Through my adolescence, I asked my parents countless times for a professional camera, and it just never really happened. Finances, discourse between my parents, blah blah blah. It just wasn't in the cards for me. So because a few girlfriends in high school had cameras and were out playing and practicing, I adopted a belief system that it was too late for me.

I wasn't even aware I adopted this belief system, but it was so deeply ingrained in me that I had amnesia towards the fact that it was something I was even interested in.

So this idea pops into my head, and I am electrified by it. I call my boyfriend, who was fully supporting us at the time, and told him verbatim, "Hey, I think I'm gonna go buy a professional camera and lens... it's gonna run us about 5k." We weren't exactly swimming in cash at this point, but because Jonathon has done years of personal development himself and is the most optimistic person I know, he encouraged me to go for it, without one second of hesitation. (Thank you for that, my love. We wouldn't be here without you.)

So I threw my son in his car seat, took off to Best Buy, charged five thousand dollars to a new credit card with zero expectations other than knowing that this is something I am interested in and I wanna try it out.

What followed were months of endless excitement, energy, and enthusiasm. I asked everyone I knew to model for me, offered every shoot for free, took to YouTube to learn how to work my camera in manual and edit in Lightroom, and played. I felt like a little freaking kid, and I was having SO much fun. There were no expectations, no perfect formula, just a new personality I was trying on—and it fit like a glove.

My art evolved quickly, and it was clear to me that I was most engaged and excited about shooting love stories. This is when I decided I WAS going to be an elopement photographer. Notice I said "was," not "wanted." 'Cause I knew it was gonna happen for me—the "how" didn't matter.

At the time, I had had my camera for about seven months. I had built a decent portfolio, had gained some actual paid clients here and there, but I was dying to shoot an elopement. I live in the wedding capital of the world. There are over three hundred weddings here every day. Surely someone would hire me to shoot their wedding, right? WRONG. The thing about photography is, until you have the work to show you can do it, no one is going to hire you to do it. Unfortunate, yes... but I was determined.

Always working on myself and my mindset, the audiobook I was listening to at this time was *You Are a Badass at Making Money*, by Jen Sincero. I was working on my money mindset, girlfriend, and you best believe I was going to make some shit happen. This didn't mean that I wasn't struggling with impostor syndrome, self-doubt, or unworthiness. There were two voices in my head through it all: One of encouragement, and one of insecurities. I just chose to lean into the positive one. I was focusing on the good.

It was December 2022, and I told myself that I was going to make $120,000 from my photography in the upcoming year, no *ifs*, *ands*, or *buts*. It was happening. I wrote it on napkins, journals, while coloring with my kids. I talked about it, told people it was happening, and acted "as if" it was going to.

So, what were some steps I took to prepare? Well, I got my LLC to become a legitimate business. I opened a business bank account so my money had somewhere to flow to. I invested in customer relationship management (CRM) software, which is designed to capture inquiries, send contracts, and keep clients and projects organized. I asked my friend to be my virtual assistant (even though I had maybe one inquiry a week and absolutely did not need her, I knew I would).

But alas, still no one would hire me for a wedding. So I decided to fake it. No one will hire me? No problem...I'll hire myself. I bought a thirty dollar wedding dress on Amazon and cute fuzzy pink heels to match the funky flair. I asked my already-married friends to model for me. I had a friend who liked to play with flowers make me a bouquet, and I took to the streets of downtown Las Vegas to shoot my shot.

My husband followed me around to capture some behind-the-scenes (BTS) footage on an iPhone, and off we went, laughing and running around in the City of Lights. I didn't know what I was doing, but I was doing it, motivated by a heavy dose of delusion and a sprinkle of false confidence that I will forever be grateful for. I couldn't get home fast enough to play with the photos and see how the work turned out.

It's important to mention that I had been on day seven of my "actually be consistent on TikTok for a month" experiment. So the very next morning, after editing some of the photos, I took to TikTok to post a few BTS clips with an overlay text that said, "POV: you elope in Las Vegas and I'm your photographer," followed by five of my favorite shots.

I didn't think anything of it and continued on with my day, but within twenty-four hours, the video had gone viral, and my business exploded. Overnight, I had received over fifty inquiries! I went from shooting ZERO weddings to shooting seven that VERY SAME WEEK. It was a complete whirlwind, followed by a lot of tears, gratitude, and a feeling of, *holy hell, this whole manifestation thing actually works.*

I am delighted to share that my projected income was 120k by March of that year, and by the end of my first year in business, I made over a quarter million. Did I mention I got pregnant with our daughter, Aria Rain, in the midst of this crazy busy year? Was it an amazing first year in business? Yes. Was it incredibly challenging? Also yes. But I did get the home birth that I had been dreaming of... that was a big win.

My life and business continue to evolve. Photography continues to electrify me, but the breadcrumbs of my life and my story are what really keep me going. A forever student and a very vulnerable teacher. I believe in miracles—and it all starts when you focus on the good.

About Mackenna

Mackenna Dugan is a Las Vegas-based wedding photographer, podcast host, and founder of *All-In Elopements*—a full-service wedding company blending high-end hospitality with heartfelt, intimate celebrations. After going viral on TikTok, she built a multiple six-figure photography business in her first year and has since helped over three hundred couples from around the world capture their love stories in iconic Vegas fashion.

She also hosts the *Focus on the Good Podcast*, where she shares insights on motherhood, mindset, women in business and building a purpose-driven life. Mackenna lives in Las Vegas with her husband, Jonathon, and their three children—raising a family and legacy rooted in service, storytelling, and chasing meaningful moments.

Instagram: @mackennadphotography @focusonthegoodpodcast @mackennadteam @allinelopements

Whatever it Takes

Mireika Edwards

Statistically speaking, I shouldn't be where I am today, and here's why.

Only fifty percent of foster children graduate high school. Fifty percent will develop substance abuse dependency. And at some point after aging out, thirty-six percent become homeless and fifty-six percent unemployed. Only three percent earn college degrees. Even after those numbers, even if you have been one of those statistics, I don't believe that being a foster child is guaranteed to define your life in a negative light. It's how you continue on after being a foster child and even after being a statistic. I come from nothing, but I've learned to move like I've always had everything. The odds are stacked against you as a ward of the state but through so much abandonment, I've built a beautifully successful life for myself.

For most of my adult life, I got to say, "I'm a model and MMA ring girl," when people asked what I did for work. I always loved the recognition of that. Instant interest beaming from their faces at me. I imagine that's the reassurance and excitement a small child gets from their parents when they sing their ABCs or learn to count. Although I don't believe that being a foster child defines you in a negative way, I know that it does define you, like the small example I mentioned. Every day, I think about it. Every day, in small ways, I'm reminded of the things I didn't get growing up: hugs, kisses, bedtime stories, or milestone markers. I have one small book of pictures of my first eight years of life. I'll never know what my first words were or what age I started walking, but I will tell you something my unique upbringing did give me. It gave me resilience, adaptability, courage, independence, and weirdly enough, outward confidence even if inwardly I struggled with wanting to be wanted.

I've often daydreamed about a life with a mom, dad, and loving siblings where we had family game night and yearly vacations, but in the midst of each cloudy "what if," I know in my heart that I wouldn't change a thing. I love my story.

My strength is worth every struggle.

I am ME, Mireika Edwards.

In my mid-twenties, I went online to explore my biological family. I learned I'm Swedish and Irish. I found a long-lost brother who is now my closest and most loving sibling. I haven't seen my biological mom since I was eight, which was twenty-five years ago, but I plan on reuniting with her soon. I don't expect much out of it. I'd like one hug, if anything. I met my biological dad once and shortly after that, he passed away. It was a strange feeling looking into familiar eyes. I'm so disconnected from my blood that I've really only seen those familiar eyes when I look in the mirror.

We didn't connect much when we met. Our humor was very different, and I got this overwhelming sense he felt guilty he didn't raise me. He thought I grew up with my mom and sounded hurt when he learned I grew up in the system. Although that day wasn't like a heartfelt Lifetime movie, I'll cherish chatting with him my entire life. He gave me a lot of insight about my mom as a younger woman.

I loved hearing stories about my mom before I was born. She has really great qualities, great qualities that I wish she used for good. Surprisingly, I learned we had some things in common. Loving our big blonde hair, almost as if it's our identity. We're charismatic communicators, energized by connection, not easily embarrassed, and even enjoy billiards at dive bars. It was sweet to learn I carry some of my mother's traits, although she is a stranger to me.

Sometimes I wonder what went wrong with the little girl inside my mom. I wonder what the defining moment was for her to be the way she is. Why she chose crime over her children. I wish I could have been there for her. Because of her mental illnesses, I'll never get the true story of her life or mine.

I do think a lot about the little girl I was, because I know her deeply and personally. I think about how much love and stability she deserved. I've sculpted myself as a woman my younger self would be proud of, and I pride myself on that daily. I will never let her down. No one can take that from us. And when sculpting yourself as an adult that your younger self would be proud of, please remember this: no one can come between you and your younger self because you share a bond. You're doing it for you— your past, present, and future self. Don't let anyone tell you who you are or have been. Only you know, and truly, that is special.

And I need to say this in the most dramatic way possible, and I mean this with my entire being. GOOD FOSTER PARENTS ARE SO IMPORTANT. Actually, good foster parents deserve to be gifted with the fullness of life's blessings. Outside of being a legal guardian, if you can just positively impact one child's life, you are deserving of heaven's richest rewards. A child only needs ONE positive role model to believe in them to succeed. We should all try to be that one.

I wouldn't be who I am today without a string of amazing foster parents and guardians. In particular, Mr. and Mrs. Shaw of Alabama and William "Bill" Miller, the legend himself. I can say with confidence that I owe them my life. "They saved me" is an understatement. I could write chapters or books about them individually. Although they are on the other side, a shout out for my success is the least I could do. And although they aren't physically here to read my chapter, I can always feel them all around me, guiding and protecting me. I really do have the most incredible guardian angels.

That leads me to my deep-rooted faith and how God has raised me since I can remember. I'll never forget being in a small Sunday school class in the south learning about Jesus for the first time. They said "Our Father," and that wasn't a light statement to me. You must know my first memories were in the system. I knew that I didn't have a mother or father. I knew my upbringing wasn't normal very early on. So, when I learned of our Father and I started seeing he was in every home I was in, I knew he was my one and only constant in my early years of childhood. When I was transferred to a new home and they prayed at dinner, or went to church, or had his picture on the wall, I would smile and know my Father was still here with me.

It comforted the small child in me all my life and it consumes me to this day. My faith is my core. I'm extremely blessed for that. I knew early in life what was important to me. Some could say I grew up too fast, but if that's all you know, how could you compare it to anything else? I wouldn't change a day.

For the future, I see a lot of doors continuing to open for me. Whether that's successfully, spiritually, or even in the doors of the hearts of people who need kindness and love. Big or small, I just want a genuine and happy life. I want to inspire, and most importantly, I want to understand others, building beautiful relationships where we can support one another deeply. We all just want to be loved and understood. We all have experienced pain and loss, where we've lost loved ones or where we experienced a period of time where we completely lost ourselves. But guess what? Our time isn't over, and we'll never hit our prime. We are forever evolving and outdoing ourselves because that's who we are.

That's what we do.

We slay.

About Mireika

Mireika Edwards is a complex woman with an unconventional upbringing,
a multi-passionate creator with a look that captivates and a story that moves hearts. She is a model, a ring girl, and an overall powerhouse of feminine strength and unstoppable grit. She has a mission to inspire foster children or those who have felt misunderstood by what their childhoods shaped them to be. From home to home, state to state, literally across the country starting as a baby, she ended up in a very small town in Nevada that she reps proudly, Pahrump. At eighteen she moved just over the hump to the big city of Las Vegas, which ultimately changed her life.

She had a salaried nine-to-five and was going to college at nineteen until she was picked up as a model and MMA ring girl, which is fitting for her as she loves most sports. MMA was always a big celebration in her hometown. Her foster dad loved sports, especially football and boxing. And without a mother figure at all, maybe the clothes and makeup didn't instantly feel familiar, but she quickly learned that modeling came naturally to her. She's loved it all for almost fifteen years now. In her twenties she had a lot of fun and was a bit wild—as she would say, maybe got "lost in the sauce"—but now in her thirties, she wants to express a genuine and honest voice that inspires others to be themselves. She craves more intentional leadership as she continues to represent brands and herself. Please join Mireika Edwards as she continues to slay the statistics.

Instagram: mireikaedwards

Neon-Lit Legacy: Megan Fazio Slays Las Vegas, One Power Move at a Time

Megan Fazio

One of the first words people use to describe me (straight to my face, even, as if it were a compliment) is *intimidating*. I sat with that descriptor for years, feeling moderately insulted and thinking it was something I could and should change. I uncomfortably forced myself to smile more, went out of my way to be kind, even to those who wouldn't reciprocate, often in a way that felt unnatural, but the word continued to stick with me.

Finally, I decided to flip the narrative on its head: *I am not intimidating; people are intimidated.*

There's a difference. I'm not mean or aggressive: I am honest and assertive, and that makes some people uncomfortable. Especially being a woman showing up in spaces predominantly dominated by men. And it's not ME that makes people uncomfortable; my PRESENCE challenges their comfort.

As I've become more comfortable in my own skin, I've come to realize why: Some people play supporting roles in their own story, but I've never been one of them. I've always known I had "main character" energy—not in a flashy or self-obsessed way, but in the grounded, get-sh*t-done, take-up-space kind of way. The kind of presence that shows up fully—heels clicking, phone buzzing, lashes curled. Always, and above all, I mean business. Whether I'm sitting in a strategy session with luxury hotel execs, walking the sidelines of an NFL game in full glam, back squatting four hundred pounds, or speaking truth into the mic on my podcast *Neon Confidential*, I do so with intention.

But make no mistake—my story isn't about the glam. It's about the grit.

As the founder and CEO of Neon PR Studios, I've spent the last decade building more than a business—I've built a brand that reflects my values: bold thinking, intentional action, and meaningful impact.

I believe my career is not about just managing accounts and shaping narratives—but shaping the future of Las Vegas hospitality and the way the world sees Las Vegas, one perfectly-crafted narrative and viral-worthy moment at a time. Neon's client roster includes some of the most iconic names in the city and reads like the A-list lineup of a luxury traveler's dream: The Bellagio, The Cosmopolitan of Las Vegas, Wynn Las Vegas, Mandalay Bay, and Resorts World—names that don't just dominate The Strip, but define it. But to me, it's not about the names; it's about the strategy, the creativity, and the magic we bring.

The Making of Neon

I didn't just waltz into this industry with a PR degree and a dream. Starting this agency wasn't easy. I didn't have a roadmap—just a relentless work ethic, a deep love for storytelling, and a refusal to accept mediocrity. Before launching my agency, I'd spent years in the PR trenches, working for other agencies, learning the business inside and out and quietly shaping a vision for what I would do differently.

When it was finally my turn, at the ripe age of twenty-four, I launched Neon PR Studios with no guarantees—just grit. Now, with nearly fifteen years of experience publicizing chefs, restaurants and lifestyle brands, we've carved out a space in one of the most competitive, fast-moving cities in the world. My team of six is behind some of the most innovative PR and social media work in hospitality. We've got our hands on the most iconic venues in Las Vegas, including the Mayfair Supper Club (yes, *that* iconic Bellagio stunner that brings Gatsby-level glam back to dining), The Vault at Bellagio (the city's most exclusive secret, now expertly unwrapped through social and PR), Bottled Blonde Las Vegas (a nightlife darling commanding the influencer spotlight), and downtown staples like Container Park, Gold Spike, and Corduroy, where culture and community collide.

It takes more than luck to thrive in Las Vegas. It takes vision—and I've held tight to mine from day one.

Opening our twenty-nine hundred-square-foot headquarters on Main Street in the burgeoning Las Vegas Arts District felt both full-circle and symbolic. I've always believed in this city, and investing in the area where culture, creativity, and entrepreneurship intersect was my way of doubling down on that belief. It wasn't just a power move or smart business decision—it was a love letter to Neon's clients and the city that raised my hustle. Every neon light in our office, every perfectly crafted campaign, every curated post infused with intention and strategy, every late-night brainstorm comes with a purpose—and a whole lot of heart.

That heart is what sets us apart.

My biggest source of pride? Relationships. While the industry is known for flash and fast turnover, I've built Neon on staying power. Over a dozen of our clients have been with us nearly a decade—proof that trust, results, and alignment speak louder than trends. That's why our clients stay. Because I'm not just selling publicity. I'm building legacies—with them, for them, and alongside them.

Nowadays, our clients' audiences are smarter, savvier, and more emotionally driven than ever before—and we meet them there, whether it's through a storytelling-forward press pitch, a viral-worthy social campaign, or a jaw-dropping influencer experience on The Strip.

Beyond the Business

What I don't talk about enough is the *why* behind all this.

I've built this life and business while navigating some really real personal growth. I've been through the kind of heartbreak that humbles you, the kind of business challenges that could bury a lesser woman, and the kind of life transitions that force you to meet your truest self. After years of personal growth and hard-won healing, I choose peace over performance, clarity over chaos, and purpose over popularity.

That means choosing peace even when it's hard. Saying "no" to opportunities that don't align, even when they're shiny. Creating space for joy and rest, even when the world glorifies hustle. And trusting that what's meant for me will find me—if I keep doing the inner and outer work.

Today, every client I take on, every project I say "yes" to, every team member I lead—it all comes from a place of alignment. I'm building a business that supports the life I want, not one that drains the life out of me.

These days, my wins feel different. Bigger, yes—but also more *aligned*. Whether meditating at sunrise, hosting a panel of powerhouse women, or brainstorming the next viral campaign for the Bellagio fountains, it all flows from the same source: intention.

I'm not chasing validation—I'm creating a legacy.

Purpose-Driven PR

I've also found power in using my platform for causes that matter. In the last few years, I've taken on clients like New Vista, Nevada Fertility Advocates, and Monday's Dark—nonprofits and collectives that are doing transformational work. It's been incredibly rewarding to shift into purpose-driven PR, where the return isn't just media impressions—it's impact. The sorts of companies aren't just checkboxes on a client list—they're causes close to the heart.

I believe advocacy and aesthetic aren't mutually exclusive—they're a powerful pair. I love luxury, and I love hospitality, but I also love *helping*. Amplifying voices that deserve to be heard. Giving visibility to causes that deserve to be seen. PR can be more than flashy campaigns and pretty pictures—it can be deeply human, too.

The Neon Confidential Era – The Power of Presence (and Platform)

A few years ago, I launched my podcast, Neon Confidential, and it's become one of my favorite creative outlets. It's where I get to pull back the curtain on what it *really* looks like to run a business, stay sane, and evolve in public. It's where I get to be unfiltered, honest, and hopefully, helpful.

Through *Neon Confidential*, I try to blend unfiltered honesty with hard-earned business wisdom, and invite listeners into my world with transparency (and a little bit of wit). I talk about the pressure, the pivots, and the behind-the-scenes messiness that doesn't make it into a client case study. And I do it because I know I'm not the only one figuring it out in real time. I don't pretend to have it all together. But I *do* have the tools, the experience, and the voice to lead with transparency—and that's what I bring to the mic.

I believe by sharing my story and other founders' stories, that I'm not just spotlighting them or myself; I'm holding up a mirror for others who are ready to own their story, their power, and their next chapter.

Redefining the Slay

People ask me all the time: "How do you do it all?"

For me, slaying isn't about always doing more—it's about doing what matters. It's about boundaries. It's about knowing your worth. It's about choosing long-term impact over short-term hype. It's about becoming the kind of woman your younger self would be proud of —and who your future self will thank you for becoming.

I used to think success was about being everywhere, doing everything, looking perfect while doing it. Now I know it's about presence. And making sure the life I'm building *feels* as good as it looks.

Success used to look like constant motion. Now, it looks like an intentional movement.

What's Next

Right now, Neon PR Studios is stepping into our most exciting season yet. And I feel it deep in my bones: this is still just the beginning.

I'm not afraid to dream bigger. I'm not afraid to pivot when needed. I'm building something lasting—something that evolves as I do.

It's not just about revenue goals, retainer clients, or being seen at the "right" events. It's about **impact**. It's about living boldly, loving intentionally, and working creatively—*without apology*. It's about using my voice, my skillset, and my platforms to **amplify authenticity** in a world that craves realness.

It's about saying *yes* to what aligns, and *no* to what drains.

It's about being the woman who can drop a jaw with a perfectly styled outfit, *and* drop a truth bomb on a strategy call with Fortune 500 execs.

It's about creating space—literal and figurative—for your team, your community, and your future self. It's about showing the world that you can be the main character and the mastermind behind the curtain.

And it's about never, ever playing small just because someone else feels uncomfortable when you shine.

I've stopped living for the "highlight reel" and started living for the real thing.

Because the real flex? Isn't the clout. Isn't the client list. It isn't even the press. It's that I've built a life and a business that aligns with *exactly who I am*.

And I'm proud of that woman. The one who never settled. The one who kept going. The one who shines out loud—and helps others do the same. And that, to me, is the ultimate flex.

That's how I slay.

About Megan

Megan Fazio is the CEO and founder of Neon PR Studios, a full-service PR and marketing firm based in Las Vegas representing hospitality, entertainment, adventure, and nonprofit clients. As a public relations business professional with several years of travel and tourism-related industries, multi-agency, high risk accounts, and nonprofit PR experience, Megan focuses on helping businesses penetrate targeted markets and attain high visibility in these markets by garnering positive buzz and media attention, but more importantly, she measures her success according to the impact she has on driving her clients' businesses forward. With nearly fifteen years of publicizing chefs, restaurants, and lifestyle clients, and profiles in MSN, *LA Weekly*, and now *USA Today* (rare for a publicist), Megan continues to lead and manage innovative communications strategies for hospitality, business, tech, and crisis management. A trusted PR advisor at the highest levels, she's led hundreds of successful media campaigns, develops strategic messaging, builds relationships, and protects brands and reputations. With Megan at the helm, Neon PR Studios has become an industry force, creating the "'it factor'" for Vegas hospitality brands like few others.

https://www.linkedin.com/in/meganfazio
https://neonprstudios.com/
Instagram: @meganfazio @neonprstudios
TikTok: @megan.fazio

Life Sucks, Then You Die

Miranda Hoover

"Life sucks, then you die."

Ten years ago, I was introduced to this quote, featured on the best bumper sticker of all time, and it still lives in the kitchen cabinet of a family friend.

At some point, we are all going to die, but the "life sucks" part? I refused to let that be my truth.

I am a former people-pleaser with a side of codependency; I have post-traumatic narcissist disorder (PTND) and am a recovering perfectionist. As the oldest of five kids, I was treated like the third parent as soon as I was old enough to understand how to change a diaper and feed a baby. My mom won't appreciate me saying that, as I can keenly remember the day when she aggressively told me I was "not the third parent." But as a therapist later pointed out, I was "over-parentified," basically the same thing. I always took care of my four younger siblings and eventually babysat for all the kids in my neighborhood, plus those of family friends.

Being the people-pleaser I was, I always had the gumption to do more, and even when I felt exhausted or overwhelmed, I pushed through and did even more. In high school, I worked two jobs, was on the student council, was a national champion with FBLA, was a member of We the People, played basketball, and was an active volunteer with Key Club. I worked three jobs to put myself through college, while taking almost twice the amount of credits per year necessary, which led me to graduate a year early, while being an elected senator for my college, then president of a college club, and active in multiple others. I looked for parental approval in everything I pursued, trying to earn acknowledgment for how hard I worked, get an "I'm proud of you" comment, and be allowed to spend time with friends or go on a class trip. After all, I was a perfectionist, and of my entire K–12 schooling, I only missed two days of school. Ever.

Since I was fourteen years old, I knew I would forge my own path and wanted to be my own boss. I had determination, resiliency, and the will to figure it out. I also cared for people deeply, often even more than myself. As I look back at the bright-eyed, bushy-tailed young woman I was, full of ambition, everyone's friend, and a hard worker, I am reminded of my strong desires for freedom. The freedom to make my own decisions, live on my own, be taken seriously, and make a difference in my community. I wanted desperately to be taken seriously and stand out from the crowd of "movers and shakers."

Little did I know that little girl would be knocked far off the path she had forged so hard for herself. When I was fifteen, I met the guy I thought I was going to marry. We started dating a week after my twenty-first birthday. I thought he was the most gorgeous man I had ever seen: he was charming, friends with everyone, and part of an affluent family in town. We dated on and off for four years. Four years of what turned me into the complete opposite person of who I was. He was a narcissistic alcoholic with a drug and gambling problem.

I look back on those four years now, and I don't even recognize the person who stared back at me in the mirror. That woman was soulless. Verbally abused and sleep-deprived from being constantly awoken in the middle of the night from a drunken yelling tantrum, criticized for every ingenuous idea and verbalized dream for the future. I became emotionless; so beaten down that nothing felt like it mattered. I kept allowing him back into my life because I believed in fighting for love and that everything worth having is worth fighting for. But this time in my life sucked. It sucked my soul, my dreams, goals, self-confidence, and individualism.

It took me a long time to realize I had the choice to decide whether I was going to allow those four years to define me or not. I was wildly unhappy, depressed, wondering if I would ever find myself again. I started listening to personal development podcasts, reading books and researching. I kept coming back to research that told me anything is possible with the right mindset. Frankly, that sounds like a load of BS when you're hearing it in the state of mind I was in. But I started working out again, eating foods that nourished my body, and listening to people who had been through similar situations. I slowly started seeing my family and friends again and learned I had post-traumatic narcissist disorder. I had been taken away from my friends and family because, as I later learned, that's how narcissists keep you entwined. I was told by my therapist how surprised she was that I hadn't fallen into the same crowd and that my actions during this time shouldn't be held against me.

That post-breakup period can best be described as a horror movie. I would travel down dark alleys and streets by myself in the middle of the night, walk past gangs of people who looked like they could snatch me up in an instant, sit in dive bars with drunken strangers, drive to the outskirts of town with no cell service, and none of it scared me. I was in search of a feeling. Acquaintances of my former boyfriend continued to contact me, asking ridiculous questions and trying to get answers from me. I cared, but I also didn't... my emotions had been pushed so far down and away that my mom later told me I wasn't even recognizable to her.

It took a lot of time and work to shift my mindset by creating goals that I knew I could achieve, trying to get back onto a path of productivity and chasing my dreams with the knowledge that I wanted more in life. Through self-work, therapy, reading, research, body movement and podcasts that I threw myself into over the last six years, it is safe to say I now know myself pretty well. I was knocked off my perfectionist pedestal hard. I was extremely bruised, and I still carry scars from that time. It's been hard to find a happy medium between perfectionism and being stuck so far down a hole that the light at the top looks like a pushpin point. But if not for that experience, I know I would still be vying for the perfectionist lifestyle: one with no breaks, time for deep reflection, or self-care, and I would still believe I could never fail hard.

The biggest mindset shift I had to make was about how to turn the once self-confident and highly ambitious person that I was back on. The answer was that I needed to first forgive myself and then forgive him, not because he deserved it, but because it's what my soul needed.

Without this experience, I'm not sure I would have made it through being personally sued, my business being sued, being told by a former employee that I have a "black heart," being completely broke and wondering how I would pay my bills, being stressed to the point of not sleeping for days, and being completely and utterly alone without help or support. I've lost multiple friends to fentanyl overdoses and helped to comfort their families. I've cared for patients at the end of their life, including my own grandfather, who I love and miss dearly. And it is because of my resilience and fervor to love harder, work harder, be better, and do good that I have gotten through everything life has thrown at me so far.

One of my superpowers is listening intently. I can discern information and give you exactly what you've asked for. Resurrecting my true self, I again look forward to helping others. Are you looking for advice? I got you. Are you looking for me to simply be silent and acknowledge what you're going through? I'm here for you. Do you need three tangible examples of how an employee that you're about to let go of may react? I've got four. Well before the popular social media trend of "we listen and we don't judge" was going around, that was my motto. People who have been through hard things will never judge someone else.

Through times of hardship and struggle, people were judgmental toward me because they couldn't understand what I was going through. I simply stopped sharing with them and actively looked to make new friends who I hoped I could relate to better. I learned that because of the parentification early on in my life and having a traumatic relationship with an older man, I was actually a fifty-year-old in a twenty-five-year-old's body. Or at least it felt that way!

These challenges led me to work with various nonprofits, engaging in servant work. I see all people, without judgment, listening to understand. I approach my work with a tenacity to fight—for myself, my family, my community, and those who cannot or do not know how to fight for themselves. Everyone deserves a chance to live a life they love, with the ones they love, regardless of circumstances. Failing and enduring hardship are good; sometimes, courage is needed to change your mindset so you can look back and valiantly declare that your life didn't suck.

About Miranda

Miranda Hoover is the founder and co-managing partner at 3C-House. A native Nevadan, she represents and advocates for companies, trade associations, and nonprofits at the local, state, and federal level. 3C-House is a full-service strategic communications firm specializing in government affairs, external affairs, crisis communications, grassroots outreach, business building, economic development, coalition building, digital marketing, and public relations.

With more than thirteen years of experience working with small businesses, elected officials, and associations and owning companies in the logistics, consulting, and lobbying industries, Miranda brings a passion for smart communication, leadership, policy, and a business growth mindset, while helping businesses start and expand. Miranda previously led the only orthopedic nonprofit for education and research in Nevada and has advocated for over twenty nonprofits and organizations with service projects, including groups that support animals, land conservation, education and scholarships, breast cancer treatment and awareness, children and literacy, and competitive sports for Special Olympics.

Miranda is currently a board member of the Western Nevada College Foundation. In 2019, she was given a Top 10 Saleswoman of the Year award and in 2024 was awarded as a 20 Under 40 by the Young Professionals Network.

Miranda received a BS in community health sciences with a minor in nutrition and criminal justice and an MPA specializing in healthcare policy and business administration from the University of Nevada. You can find her spending time with her family and her chug, Onyx, and enjoying a meal and drink at a local establishment with friends and fellow thought leaders.

Instagram: @miranda.m.hoover @3chousenv
www.3chousenv.com

From Hopeless to Hope-Filled: Healing & Helping Others Find Their Way

Tabitha Johnson

When I arrived on the scene as a mental health therapist in Grace City, I wasn't sure what to expect. I was surprised to find myself intrigued by the people who live here. Their stories were often riddled with pain and struggle, but what I found was that purpose unfolded. I would like to share one of the cases I came to know more intimately.

Presentation

The client presents as a forty-six-and-a-half-year-old African American female. She is divorced, has two children, a boy, age fifteen, and a girl, age twelve. She was raised by her mother (Caucasian) and stepfather (Ghanaian) along with her brother, who is nine years her junior. She had another brother, from Kenya, who searched for her online for six years, and they met for the first time when she was twenty-eight. She was then reunited with her biological father two years later, and took a trip to Kenya, where she met her other siblings (ten). Medically, she has had two C-sections, with a significant loss of blood during her second pregnancy, which required several blood transfusions. She had gastric sleeve surgery in 2017 and has been able to keep off one hundred pounds since the surgery.

The client came in originally for services as she was having difficulty with her identity and self-worth. She learned at age seven that, due to certain family members having concerns with a biracial child being born into the family, that her mother should give her up for adoption. Her mother did decide to go through with the pregnancy and keep her, despite the controversy in the family.

She presents with anxiety and depression, insomnia, as well as symptoms related to posttraumatic stress disorder, such as flashbacks, nightmares, and hypervigilance. She is high-functioning, and has been able to sustain employment in various leadership positions.

The client reports concerns related to having a healthy relationship with a partner, given her history of often choosing partners who have their own unhealed trauma, or who are emotionally unavailable. She also has concerns of codependency, given her desire to feel loved and worthy of a partner's affections, even when she recognizes that the relationship may be unhealthy. Her goal is to finally feel worthy of loving herself, and to heal the childhood wounds of understanding that she was initially not wanted in this world. The client reports having these concerns since her teenage years, and had periods of time where self-harm was present. She reports no suicidal ideation or self-harm at this time.

Predisposing Factors

The client appears vulnerable to feeling judged by others in her life. She appears to seek approval and often seeks out performance-based activities to feel comfortable in her own skin. She reports having two parents who had a strong work ethic and believed in the value of higher education. She sought out two master's degrees and continues to further her learning in her field.

She reports several traumas: the recent death of her brother, who had searched for her for six years and died of stage IV colon cancer; the divorce of her partner of twenty-one years; and having been in an unhealthy relationship that involved emotional abuse, verbal threats, and being illegally locked out of her own home. Through the generosity of those in her support system, she was able to stay safely with friends at that time, while she secured permanent housing for herself and her children.

The client has a history of trusting people easily and being a "people pleaser." She has been working through her need to be liked and accepted by others. She reports growing up in a household where certain cultural norms often minimized the voice of the females in the family.

Precipitating Factors

The client has been working through the various losses that she has experienced. In addition, she indicates that she is attempting to rebuild herself financially in order to purchase a home for herself and her children. She reports stress from a new job and being the sole provider in the household as a precipitating factor.

The divorce appears to have created strain in her family of origin. She is estranged from her family, as they reportedly disagreed with her filing for divorce. Her current support system consists primarily of friends, both local and from out of state, who give her an outlet to share her worries, fears, and frustrations.

Patterns

The client is active, and enjoys running and going to the gym; she knows these are healthy activities and spaces for her when she is feeling anxious or stressed. She often notes that she has felt a great deal of shame, both publicly and personally, due to several of the recent traumas.

The client indicates that she uses work as a way to cope, and in addition to her full-time job, she runs two small businesses. She also reports feeling guilty for how much she works, but that she is working toward a goal of owning a home and has two children in private school.

Perpetuating Factors

The client reports that she has often held onto certain family and personal relationships, even if they were unhealthy for her. She sought to "keep the peace," and now recognizes the emotional cost that this has had.

She recognizes that cognitive distortion—the idea that she is not able to be loved—has held her back from living her life fully and completely. The client recognizes that her avoidance of dealing with these feelings, on a real level, keeps her stuck and unable to move forward in an authentic way. Prior to weight loss surgery, the client reports that food was her main coping mechanism for dealing with any negative emotion. This led to years of battling with her weight. As she is unable to cope in the same way with food, she now has to face these emotions.

The client reports shame in not being able to recognize and identify negative relational patterns in her own relationships, as she is trained to do so in her profession. She is learning to see that despite her training, she is only human.

Protective Factors and Strengths

Though the client presents with both childhood and adult trauma, and an ACES (adverse childhood experiences) score of five, she reports having a significant faith. She states that she is a Christian, was baptized in 2007, and that her relationship with God has helped her to understand who she is and "Whose" she is. She recognizes that her family, like all families, has individuals who have not done their own healing. She is learning to love those people from a distance, and is not coming from a place of blame, but rather a place of cautious optimism. She notes having had several people throughout her life who were able to provide emotionally safe environments where she felt comfortable in being able to show her authentic self.

The client shares that her sense of humor is a strength. She reports being able to laugh about some of the mistakes that she has made, and often views these mistakes as learning experiences. She reports having clung to an idea of perfection and now knows that this is not possible. She is able to give herself and others grace.

The client has a positive co-parenting relationship with her ex-husband and a robust support system of people who not only love on her, but her children as well. She indicates that in addition to therapy, she sought medication management to find the medication that works for her to manage her anxiety. She began taking medication over a year ago, and this has helped decrease her anxiety significantly.

Plans

The client plans to continue to help others find their way. She knows what it is like to have no hope and to feel unloved. She now has hope and recognizes that she has a future, and that all of her tears were not wasted. She now owns her own home and is creating a space for her two children to be able to share their emotions freely. She plans to contribute to *Slaying Vegas*, and to be a light to those in her community and beyond.

The client—is me. Thank you for letting me share.

About Tabitha

Ms. Tabitha Johnson is a licensed marriage and family therapist and licensed clinical alcohol and drug counselor and

NAMI (National Alliance on Mental Illness) board member. She is passionate about helping others find their way through difficult experiences. She is certified in a type of therapy, called EMDR (Eye Movement Desensitization and Reprocessing), that addresses unprocessed trauma in the body.

Ms. Johnson has worked in a variety of behavioral health settings, such as inpatient and outpatient, for-profit and nonprofit. She has had the privilege of leading various behavioral health teams and supervising MFT (marriage and family therapist) and CPC (clinical professional counseling) interns who are seeking licensure. While practicing, Ms. Johnson enjoys working with all age groups and populations. A mother of two, and now a single mother, Ms. Johnson understands firsthand the complexities and challenges faced by many of her clients. Ms. Johnson advocates for herself and others to maintain their self-care. One of the ways she does this is by continuing to be a client in therapy.

After having weight loss surgery, Ms. Johnson became a certified health and life coach. She works with pre- and post-bariatric surgery patients on creating a healthy mindset around food and their bodies.

Ms. Johnson is a published author of a children's book, *Tabby Gets Her Feelings Out.* She aims to normalize the topic of mental health, to include therapy and medication. She enjoys collaborating with like-minded individuals and is excited to Slay Vegas and beyond.

Instagram: @gabwithtab or @therealbariboss

The Stuttering Girl Who Learned To Sell

Erica LeMarr

Erica LeMarr's story isn't a straight line to success: it's a jagged path of perseverance, grit, and purpose. Before she sold a single home, before the cameras, confidence, and social media presence, Erica walked through the kind of darkness that either breaks you or builds you.

The truth is, even her family predicted she would be dead in a ditch somewhere one day. She wasn't supposed to "make it." Not even close.

Raised in a home marked by instability, Erica experienced firsthand the confusion and emotional distance that followed two divorces. Her biological father was absent, and her stepfather couldn't understand her. From a young age, she was diagnosed with chronic attention deficit hyperactivity disorder, as well as a significant stuttering speech impediment, making learning and communication difficult. She had a major learning disability and was placed in special education classes, where she often felt overlooked. But even then, there was a sense stirring inside her, a quiet conviction that her life was meant for something more.

At the age of ten, while living with her family in Okinawa, Japan, on an Air Force base, Erica made a discovery: she found herself captivated by Pokémon cards. However, she didn't have the money to buy them, and her mother couldn't afford to give her any additional allowance, money which was already spread between her and her three younger sisters.

Instead, her mother offered her something else: the opportunity to earn it. Erica accepted that challenge and turned it into her first business. Determined to find a way to make more money to appease her (mild) obsession, she thought about a problem she could solve that people lacked the time to do, and decided on a dog walking service. She walked her neighborhood, knocked on twenty-five doors, and secured ten loyal dog-walking customers. For two years, she maintained that business with consistency and professionalism, learning early what it meant to build trust, solve problems, and provide value.

When the family moved to Nevada, Erica again found herself an outsider. She was socially awkward, misread, and felt like she was not understood. But she had begun developing an internal framework that no one could see—which was also a way to break free of her identity crisis.

At fifteen, in a bold act of self-definition, she invested the money she had saved from her dog walking business in Japan, gave away her current wardrobe and replaced it with all professional business attire. She wore blazers, slacks, and collared button-ups to school every day, not because she had to, but because she wanted to live in the moments that she had always dreamed of, to be a businesswoman. Most importantly, she knew even then that appearance was a part of building a presence.

Adulthood came with more lessons, many of them difficult. Erica entered a season of addiction and emotional disarray. But even in her lowest moments, she knew that she was meant for more. Call it a whisper if you will. That whisper grew louder when she met her husband, a man who saw in her what others didn't. With his support, Erica found the safe space to rebuild, this time with a focus on growth and purpose. At twenty-five, she and her husband had their son. After staying home with their son for six months, she realized that they were in a financial crisis, and decided to go back to work. The only jobs she had ever had were customer service-based positions. But she "rage applied" to different companies in an effort to bring in income and help her husband pay the bills.

She took a job in inbound sales at a major cable company. Erica had no formal background in sales and was handed a company script. But it didn't resonate with her. Instead of repeating lines, she studied behavior of the customers over the phone. She listened. She learned how people thought and made decisions. She began crafting her own approach. Within six months, she was among the top-performing salespeople in the company.

When the company launched a new product, no one quite knew how to position or sell it. Erica leaned in and studied the product benefits. She created her pitch. In less three months of the product being launched, Erica became one of the company's top salespeople in the country for that product.

This was about more than performance; it was proof of her ability to create systems, understand human motivation, and deliver results under pressure.

Despite her achievements, Erica hit a ceiling. She was asked to write the sales training protocol for the company's new offerings, but she wasn't invited to teach it. Her voice and leadership weren't part of the plan. That was her moment of clarity. She didn't want to be used for her output and excluded from the vision. She wanted to build something of her own.

A colleague who had watched her growth encouraged her to consider real estate. At first, it seemed like a stretch. She had no license, no savings, and no experience. But she had one thing that mattered: commitment. So she quit her job in an effort to "burn the boat." She failed the licensing exam four times. On the fifth, she passed. And then she did what she always did: she went all in.

In her first year, Erica sold twenty-eight homes. She quickly ranked among the top hundred agents at her company. By the next year, she had moved to a top-performing brokerage, joined the ranks of the top ten, and eventually earned the title of number one independent agent in

2022.

But Erica's story wasn't about real estate. Real estate was the platform, not the purpose.

As she continued building her business, Erica became increasingly aware that her true calling was beyond sales. It was about leadership. Specifically, it was about helping other women rise. She saw the same confusion and doubt in others that she once lived through. She began coaching female entrepreneurs, women who had the talent and drive but lacked the confidence, clarity and understanding around social media and brand building to develop their own presence.

She believes that sales and brand building are some of the most powerful tools a woman can master. Sales teaches communication, persuasion, confidence, and resilience, and brand building fosters trust and reliability. These aren't just professional skills; they are leadership traits.

Erica is on a path to teach women how to connect their gifts with their message, and how to share that message boldly, clearly, and with conviction.

Her coaching programs focus on the fundamentals that most overlook: how to master tonality, how to build presence, how to negotiate with integrity, and how to be heard. Not just in business, but in life. She teaches that confidence isn't a trait; it's a decision. That clarity doesn't come from more knowledge; it comes from trusting your voice and execution, even if it is not perfect.

Erica's work is grounded in her faith. One of her favorite scriptures is the Parable of the Talents from the New Testament. In that story, the servant who buried his gift lost everything. Erica believes that too many women are burying their gifts out of fear, doubt, or lack of support. Her mission is to help women dig them up, dust them off, and share their talents with the world.

She reminds her clients that their voice could be the very thing someone else needs to hear. That their brand isn't just a business, it's a calling. That their presence in the marketplace is not accidental, but a divine assignment.

Her coaching goes beyond surface-level strategy. She equips her clients with the tools to create consistency, maintain a strong work ethic, and show up, even when doubt creeps in. She believes in making business simple, not overwhelming. Her gift is breaking down complex ideas into steps that feel actionable and clear. She makes transformation practical.

Erica works with women who are building brands, launching products, and designing the lives of their dreams. But more than that, she works with women who are stepping into their authority, many for the first time.

Through one-on-one coaching, group intensives, and speaking engagements hosted through her vision board masterminds designed for women to create their vision boards, accompanied by a well-curated action plan which uses reverse engineering, Erica has created a space where women are seen, strengthened, and stretched. She's not interested in hype or flash. Her focus is on impact.

Erica LeMarr is no longer the girl who didn't fit. She's a voice for women who are learning to trust their own. She's building more than a business. She's building a legacy. And for her, this is only the beginning.

About Erica

Although Erica LeMarr started out with ZERO sales experience, she quickly became a top sales leader in her first sales job at a cable company, demonstrating that sales is a transferable and teachable skill.

Now, as an elite real estate professional in Las Vegas, she brings that passion for sales and faith-based principles to women across the nation, helping women forge a legacy of faith and quality influence.

Erica teaches women how social media can be their most powerful tool to amplify their voices, build their businesses, and create lasting change—not just in their businesses, but in the lives of others.

Instagram: @ericalemarrhomes

From Pain to Purpose: How I'm Leaving My Mark

Natasha Mosby

I never imagined that a one-way Greyhound ticket from Mississippi to Las Vegas would be the first step in becoming a woman called to heal others while healing herself. That long, uncertain ride wasn't just a relocation; it was the beginning of me finding my voice. My life has been shaped by faith, pain, purpose, and the unwavering belief of one woman: my mother. Through every hardship, I have learned that our deepest wounds often become the foundation for our most impactful work. This is the story of how I've transformed personal pain into purpose and left a mark not only in my profession but also in the lives of those I serve.

We moved to Las Vegas when I was going into the fifth grade. The culture shock was immediate. The people, the school system, even the way the teachers spoke—all of it felt foreign. I struggled to adjust and became withdrawn, quiet, and hesitant to engage in class. One day, my school contacted my mother to suggest I be assessed for special education. They claimed I was defiant, unwilling to participate, and not completing my work. What they didn't understand then and what I've come to realize years later was that I was experiencing adjustment disorder. What they saw as defiance was actually the early stages of anxiety and depression.

That meeting with the school is etched in my memory. My mother arrived armed with every report card from Mississippi. She wasn't there to agree; she was there to advocate. When the facilitator pushed for her to sign the paperwork, my mother picked up the pen and wrote, "Put your child in those classes," while repeating, "My daughter is capable and will succeed at anything she sets her mind to achieve." Then she looked at me and said, "Let's go, Tot." In that moment, I had my first and certainly not the last glimpse of a woman who believed and spoke life into her child, me. Her daughter. The daughter she had birthed as a teen.

My mother became my first interventionist and my greatest advocate. Because of her faith in me, God's grace and the dreams that were planted waiting on me to birth them, I went on to graduate from high school with honors and as the senior class vice president. I earned my bachelor's and master's degrees with honors, and today I'm completing my Ph.D. in health psychology. But those academic accomplishments are just the surface. What matters most is how I've used my lived experiences of loss, motherhood, divorce, and trauma to build spaces of hope and healing.

When I launched my private practice, Health, Wellness & Integrated Care, I knew I wasn't just building a business; I was creating a sanctuary. As a divorced Black woman, mother, daughter, wife, I've lived through the gaps in access to care. I've felt what it means to carry burdens silently. So I created a practice where others could be seen, heard, and supported without judgment. I integrated faith, culture, and clinical tools to help clients navigate life with dignity, hope, love, and resiliency.

My journey also led me to found and host Nevada's first free Men's Mental Health and Wellness Conference, a space to uplift a population too often expected to stay silent about their struggles. That initiative earned a proclamation from the City of Las Vegas, declaring June as Men's Health Month.

As the Clinical Program Director of the Nevada Pediatric Mental Health Access Program at the Kirk Kerkorian School of Medicine, I lead efforts to integrate mental health services into pediatric primary care across the state. I've served as a lecturer and Integrated Healthcare Program Coordinator at UNLV for nearly a decade, preparing future social workers for whole-person care. I also consult with Special Olympics Nevada, where I created the K–12 Mindset Matters program to help students manage their mental health in school settings.

But beyond the titles and roles, I'm also a mother learning how to raise whole children after divorce. I've cried behind closed doors, prayed in parking lots before work, and showed up even when my heart was heavy, but I knew God was also present. Through all of it, I've tried to model what resilience looks like, imperfect, but rooted in love, prayer, and purpose. I talk about these things openly on social media because I believe vulnerability is part of the healing. My posts reflect the real and raw parts of life, joy, pain, motherhood, faith, and mental wellness.

From that little girl who was once mislabeled to the woman leading statewide mental health programs, I've learned that the mark we leave is not in the awards we earn but in the lives we touch. My journey has taught me that healing isn't linear and that sometimes your calling is hidden in your crisis. My pain has been personal, generational, and professional, and these painful lived experiences birthed programs, opened doors, and bridged gaps in mental health access.

I am my mother's legacy, and her words continue to guide me: "My daughter is capable and will succeed at anything she sets her mind to achieve."

That's how I've found the strength to keep going. That's the deeper truth I want to share.

This is my mark. This is my mission. And this is just the beginning.

About Natasha

Natasha Mosby, LCSW, is the clinical program director of the Nevada Pediatric Mental Health Access Program with the Kirk Kerkorian School of Medicine's Department of Psychiatry and Behavioral Health. Previously, she was a lecturer and the integrated healthcare program coordinator at UNLV's School of Social Work for nine years. In her current role, Natasha leads initiatives to integrate mental health care into pediatric medical practices statewide through innovative healthcare models.

With over twenty years of experience in mental health, she is a recognized clinical expert at the University of Nevada, Las Vegas (UNLV). Her specialties include anxiety, trauma, stress-related disorders, depression, and children's mental health with a focus on integrated healthcare, bridging physical and mental healthcare delivery.

Natasha holds a master of social work from Louisiana State University and a bachelor's degree in sociology, along with an associate's degree in criminal justice, from Southern University and A&M College. Currently, she is a Ph.D. candidate in health psychology, expecting to defend her dissertation in the summer of 2025.

She is the owner and founder of Health, Wellness & Integrated Care, a boutique private practice in Las Vegas where she provides therapy, clinical consultation services, and clinical supervision. Natasha is also a sought-after consultant, offering mental health training and clinical consultation across Southern and Northern Nevada.

In 2022, Natasha planned and organized the first free Men's Mental Health and Wellness Conference in Las Vegas, focusing on men's health disparities. This annual event led to the City of Las Vegas proclaiming June as Men's Health Month. That same year, she began her second appointed four-year term as a commissioner on the Nevada Commission on Behavioral Health Board.

Additionally, Natasha serves as an advisory board member for the West Las Vegas Promise Neighborhood Maternal-Child Community Advisory Board. In 2023, she received another appointed position as the clinical consultant for Special Olympics Nevada, where she developed and oversees the K–12 Mindset Matters Mental Health Program, which helps students in the Clark and Washoe County School Districts manage stress and mental health challenges.

In recognition of her significant contributions to the City of Las Vegas, Natasha received the Women of Impact Award in 2024. While Natasha leads a busy professional life, her favorite role is being a mom. She cherishes spending quality time with her children, close friends, and family and finds fulfillment in moments of rest, reflection, and stillness.

Instagram: @ healthandwellness_nsmlcsw

Forged by Adversity, Fueled by Ambition

Donna Lisa Murray

As I write this chapter, I feel it's important to share my upbringing to help you better understand the foundation behind why I do what I do.

I was born and raised in Southern California in a strict Filipino household, deeply shaped by the values and traditions my parents brought with them when they immigrated to the United States as teenagers. They met in Hawaii while my father was serving in the Navy and my mother was living with family. Eventually, my dad was stationed in San Diego, and my mom moved to the Coachella Valley to live with her parents. After completing his service, my father joined her in the desert, where they got married and began their life together. That's where my brother and I grew up.

My parents' journey into business was built on sacrifice, grit, and vision. My mom came from a family of agricultural workers—her parents and siblings worked in the fields picking and packing produce. When babysitters weren't available, my cousins and I were brought along. My father juggled various night jobs while attending school for horticulture. He eventually secured a position at the local water district and worked his way up to supervisor. My mom earned her cosmetology license and began working at a local salon. Eventually, my parents bought that salon, marking their first big step into entrepreneurship.

From an early age, my brother and I were taught the value of hard work, discipline, and financial responsibility. My parents were incredibly frugal, choosing to purchase their first home in a low-income community not because they lacked ambition, but because they saw it as a stepping stone. Their mindset paid off: by the time I was a high school senior, they had saved enough to purchase a Fantastic Sams franchise.

After graduating in 1993, we made a bold move to Oahu, Hawaii, where my parents opened their franchise in a fast-growing area. My brother and I helped manage the salon and even attended barber styling school to better understand the business. Within two years, we were ranked in the top ten out of fifteen hundred franchises nationwide, and we stayed in the top five for years. While the business was thriving, I felt called in a different direction and decided to go back to school to study business management. My brother continued managing the salon until we sold it in 2015, as my mother's battle with breast cancer came to an end.

In 2000, I stepped away from the family business and moved back to Southern California with my then-husband to raise our growing family. After our second child was born in 2003, we opened a coffee shop in downtown San Diego. It was a rewarding experience, but running a business while raising small children proved overwhelming. We closed the shop after a year, and I transitioned into being a full-time stay-at-home mom. We settled in Murrieta and welcomed our third child in 2006. To stay connected and productive, I sold Cookie Lee jewelry, Creative Memories scrapbooking supplies, and health supplements. These side ventures helped me stay engaged and strengthened my entrepreneurial mindset.

In 2007, we moved to Las Vegas and worked opposite shifts to care for our children. By 2009, we made the tough decision to divorce. He returned to San Diego, and I chose to stay in Las Vegas to create a stable life and build my own career. It wasn't easy being a single mom with three kids under the age of seven. With no family nearby, I leaned heavily on friendships from work, especially when my children got sick or needed last-minute care.

Starting over in a new city and entering the fast-paced hospitality and convention world was intimidating. I dove in, learning the history of Las Vegas, the key hotel groups, and the massive trade shows that drive its economy. I began as a coordinator and gradually worked my way up to a sales manager, always striving for a senior or national role. In 2013, I met my husband, and we married in 2016. From the beginning, he understood the challenges I faced as a single mom and stepped in to help, preparing family dinners and supporting our routines so I could manage soccer and gymnastics practices and find balance at home.

As my kids grew older and more independent, I finally had the flexibility to attend evening networking events. That changed everything. I made meaningful connections that helped me grow professionally and opened doors I hadn't imagined. *"Your network is your net worth"* became more than a saying—it was a strategy. I joined industry committees and associations, and the time I spent volunteering helped me build relationships and credibility. I began to see that these experiences were laying the foundation for something I would one day build on my own

When the world shut down in 2020, I—like so many others—suddenly found myself without a job. My oldest daughter graduated virtually and left for college to play soccer, but the restrictions made it a difficult first year. Instead of waiting for a call back to work, I used the time to reflect. I knew this wasn't just a short pause. I enrolled in real estate classes and earned my license by August 2020. Shortly after that time, I was invited back into the event world to help rebuild our sales team and restructure processes for a post-pandemic market.

I also decided to finally launch the podcast I had been talking about for two years, highlighting stories of local entrepreneurs and professionals. By mid-2021, trade shows were back, and events had resumed at full capacity. My son graduated with a modified in-person ceremony, and life finally felt like it was returning to normal.

Then, in August 2021, everything changed again—I was diagnosed with stage 2 breast cancer. Because of my mother's history, I had mentally prepared for the possibility, but I didn't expect it so soon. I tested positive for the BRCA2 gene and quickly began treatment. I underwent a double mastectomy, chemotherapy and radiation, and a year later, I had a hysterectomy. Just as my career was gaining momentum, I was forced to stop and focus on healing. But that pause reminded me of what really matters—my health, my peace, and my family.

After my recovery, I made a conscious decision to slow down. I turned down a promotion to be more present for my youngest daughter, who was going through a difficult time as a teenager. I began stepping back from the associations I had been heavily involved with to reclaim my time and energy. During that season, I reconnected with a former colleague who had built a successful women's networking group called *Heels and Handshakes* in Nashville and Chicago. We decided to launch a Las Vegas chapter—one that aligned with my passion for building authentic connections and supporting women in business.

After our chapter launch in March 2025, I realized just how much we had been missing a community like this. The energy in the room was electric—uplifting, inspiring, and genuinely refreshing. It's rare to be in a space where women aren't competing, but instead are celebrating and uplifting one another. This is just the beginning, and I'm excited to see how far this community will grow in the years ahead.

If you doubt yourself or wonder whether you have what it takes to start something new or be your own boss, let this be your sign: just start. You don't need to have it all figured out— what matters is taking that first step. The longer you wait, the longer you delay the life you deserve. Progress begins with action, and the best time to begin is now.

About Donna

Donna Lisa Murray is the force behind the Heels & Handshakes Las Vegas Chapter, a dynamic women's networking group making major waves in the city. With over twenty years in hospitality and special events, she actively connects with hospitality students to mentor the future leaders of the industry. She's a breast cancer survivor and podcast host for Anything and Everything with Donna Lisa, highlighting local entrepreneurs and their journey in business.

She was a 2024 Smart Women in Meetings honoree and is passionate about empowering women to lead with authenticity and heart.

Instagram: @donnalisaofficial @heelsandhandshakes_vegas
Facebook: Donna Lisa Murray
Linkedin: Donna Lisa Murray

www.donnalisamurray.com

Womanhood, Work, and the Power of a Great Lipstick

Dr. Tati Pilosyan

Chapter 1: Christmas in Hollywood (No, Not the Glamorous Kind)

I was born in Yerevan, Armenia to a 23-year-old mother and father. One year into my life, the winds of change (and a very lucky immigration lottery ticket) swept through our family. My maternal grandfather—resourceful, stubborn, and probably part superhero—won the U.S. immigration lottery. He sold everything he owned, including the house he built with his own two hands, to move all of us—his wife, four daughters, their husbands, and a grandchild (me!)—to America in pursuit of the "American Dream."

We landed in the United States on Christmas Day 1990. Cue the sleigh bells... if by sleigh you mean economy seats and by bells you mean the sound of babies crying and relatives arguing over luggage.

Our new life began in Hollywood. Not the red carpet kind—unless the carpet was patterned linoleum in a cousin's one-bedroom apartment. We crammed into whatever space we could find, slept on couches, and lived like sardines—but hopeful sardines.

Chapter 2: Mama Was a Rolling Stone (With a Mop and a Dream)

When I was three, my father left. My mother became a single mom overnight, with no support, a nursing degree that didn't transfer, and a daughter with a flair for asking "Why?" four hundred times a day.

She cleaned houses, baked pastries for local shops, and made jewelry molds for Armenian jewelers in L.A.—all while taking community college classes at night to reclaim her RN license. If there were 36 hours in a day, she would've filled them.

I often went to class with her. Professors would give me "homework" to keep me occupied (or quiet), and looking back, those were probably my first baby steps into the world of healthcare. I was a tiny sidekick to a woman juggling five lives at once, and I thought that was just... normal.

Lesson #1: Never underestimate a woman with a dream, a to-do list, and access to community college.

Chapter 3: Tooth Fairy in Training (But Not Yet)

I didn't grow up thinking I wanted to be a dentist. In fact, for the longest time, I was convinced I'd become an attorney. I spent two years of high school shadowing a female judge. She was sharp, brilliant, and had a desk so covered in legal paperwork it looked like a fire hazard.

But after watching her stress levels and realizing the entire legal profession was basically endless reading and writing (my least favorite activities), I thought, "Oh no. This is not my happily-ever-after."

That realization sent me into a temporary spiral of "What am I even doing with my life?" The answer came during a high school budgeting project, where we had to pick a profession that could actually pay the bills. Dentistry checked a lot of boxes: science-based, hands-on, decent pay, and—bonus—I wouldn't have to be on call delivering babies at three a.m.

Lesson #2: Sometimes your calling finds you... through Microsoft Excel.

Chapter 4: Nerd Mode Activated

Once I decided on dentistry, I went all in. I majored in cell and molecular biology and made it my full-time job to impress admissions committees. I was the president of clubs, volunteered anywhere that would let me in, and did research in a chemistry lab where I inhaled more ethanol than I care to admit.

During my freshman year, I tracked down a professor who taught at both my university and University of California, Los

Angeles, Dental School. I emailed him (read: borderline harassed him) until he agreed to meet me. During our one-hour meeting, he gave me a piece of advice I'll never forget: "Now is the time to keep your head down and do the hard work."

So I did. While my friends were out partying, I was in the library with three-day-old coffee and a highlighter addiction. I didn't step foot into a nightclub until I was in my thirties. And honestly? Worth it.

Lesson #3: Hustle beats hype. Every. Single. Time.

Chapter 5: Dentist. USC Trained. Vegas Bound.

I got into University of Southern California Dental School, and four years later, degree in hand, I started job hunting. I didn't have any dental family connections, so I applied everywhere. A great opportunity came up in Las Vegas, and my husband and I packed our lives into a moving van and headed into the desert, planning to stay "just a few years."

Spoiler: We never left.

Vegas grew on us. My husband got into med school here, and we found our people. He started as a contractor when we met—I was just seventeen!—but pivoted into medicine. Watching him reinvent himself reminded me that it's never too late to start over, especially when you've got someone cheering you on from the sidelines (and occasionally helping you study for anatomy exams).

Lesson #4: Your path doesn't have to be linear—zigzags build character.

Chapter 6: From Tooth Rookie to Aesthetic Junkie

Four years into my career, I started exploring advanced continuing education. One day, a dentist I admired on Instagram hosted a giveaway for a conference called the Dental Influencers Alliance (DIA). I entered, forgot about it, and weeks later—surprise!—I won.

That conference changed everything. It introduced me to mentors, peers, and courses I didn't even know existed. Soon after, I enrolled in the Aesthetic Advantage program at New

York University. I flew back and forth for four years, treating real veneer cases with real patients under the guidance of top instructors.

Each time I came back from New York, I had a renewed vision of the kind of practice I wanted to build. One that was thoughtful. Elevated. Patient-centered. One that combined science with art.

Lesson #5: When you find what lights you up, follow it. Even if it flies you across the country multiple times a year.

Chapter 7: The Night Shift Dental Hustle

Around that time, the office I worked for was bought out by a corporation. Overnight, it went from a dental practice to a business. Quotas, production charts, rushed appointments—my soul shriveled a little.

I knew I needed to do dentistry my way, so I rented space from an endodontist, Dr. Scott Biggs. It was supposed to be temporary—six months, max—while I purchased my own practice.

That "six months" turned into three-and-a-half years.

We worked weekends and nights—sometimes seeing patients at ten p.m. My car became a mobile dental unit packed with supplies. We'd set up every morning and pack up every night. It was chaos. It was exhausting. And it was absolutely glorious.

My team? All women. All brilliant. All crazy enough to work full-time jobs by day and run a second practice by night. We shared snacks, tears, vent sessions, and victories. We were exhausted and inspired and utterly unstoppable.

Lesson #6: Behind every bold woman is a team of other bold women willing to grind through it with her.

Chapter 8: Building the Dream (With Blood, Sweat, and Costco Sheet Cake)

During our "temporary" years, I searched relentlessly for the perfect space to launch my own startup. Most places were either too big, too small, or priced like they came with beachfront property. After two-and-a-half years, I finally found the one. It was a bit over budget, so both my parents and in-laws pitched in.

Did I cry? Yes. Multiple times. Especially during construction. But after a year of build-out, I finally opened the doors to my very own dental sanctuary.

This wasn't just a clinic—it was the physical embodiment of every late-night study session, every patient we saw after hours, and every woman who ever dared to build her own table instead of asking for a seat.

Lesson #7: Dreams are expensive. Not just in money, but in sweat equity. But they're worth every aching muscle and meltdown.

Chapter 9: Dentistry, But Make It Meaningful

Today, I practice aesthetic dentistry with a passion that didn't exist in my early years. Back then, I liked dentistry. Now, I love it.

My favorite part? Watching patients transform. People come in hiding their smiles, and they leave standing taller and radiating confidence. It's not about the teeth—it's about the life those teeth unlock.

My practice was built on word-of-mouth referrals, which is the biggest compliment I could ever receive. People trust us. And that trust is something I will never take for granted.

Lesson #8: True success is when your work walks into a room before you do—in someone else's smile.

———

Final Thoughts

Being raised by a single mother taught me the truest definition of womanhood: resilience. Grace under pressure. A refusal to give up, even when the odds are stacked against you. I watched my mom do everything—and I never once thought a woman couldn't.

Entrepreneurship, like womanhood, is messy, magical, and almost never goes to plan. You'll lose sleep. You'll cry in your car. You'll probably question every decision. But you'll also build something that's entirely your own.

To every woman out there with a dream: keep your head down and do the hard work. But don't forget to laugh, to wear the lipstick, and to lift other women along the way.

Lesson #9: You can be soft and strong, messy and masterful, exhausted and exhilarating—all in the same breath.

Because if I've learned anything, it's this:

Hard work doesn't just build a career—it builds a life.

About Dr. Tati

Dr. Tati Pilosyan is a Las Vegas-based dentist, entrepreneur, and accidental expert in mobile dentistry (her car was once eighty percent dental supplies, twenty percent actual car). Born in Yerevan, Armenia, and raised in Los Angeles by a superhero single mom and a village of loving grandparents, she learned early that hard work, hustle, and a sense of humor are non-negotiables in life.

She originally dreamed of becoming a glamorous lawyer—until she shadowed one and realized it was mostly paperwork and stress wrinkles. A high school budgeting exercise and a very persuasive female dentist helped her pivot to dentistry, where she found the perfect mix of science, artistry, and purpose. She earned her DDS from USC and went on to complete advanced training in aesthetic and functional dentistry at NYU, where she fell in love with transforming smiles—and, in turn, transforming lives.

Dr. Tati built her practice from the ground up, literally—starting out by moonlighting in borrowed office space on nights and weekends while hauling gear like a dental Sherpa. Her boutique practice now reflects her philosophy: excellence in care, a warm patient experience, and a dash of sparkle.

Beyond the op, she's a fierce advocate for women in healthcare, passionate about entrepreneurship, and deeply committed to helping others write their own immigrant success stories.

She lives in Las Vegas with her husband, a former contractor turned medical student, and their two deeply spoiled dogs—who, thankfully, don't need veneers.

Instagram: @dr.tati.p
www.drtati.com
https://www.lasvegasaestheticdentistry.com/schedule-a-consultation

From Stage Lights to Stardust: Living the Fairytale in Vegas

Tawny Triska Pollard

Dearest reader,

Every fairytale begins somewhere—mine started in Southern California. I was an only child with a love for music, a flair for the dramatic, and the world's most supportive parents. My mom recognized my creative spark early on and gently nudged me toward the stage. By four, I was performing. By ten, I was singing Italian arias and studying classical voice. And by high school, I was winning vocal competitions and flirting with a Juilliard-bound path.

But in the early 2000s, opera wasn't exactly "cool"—especially for a fourteen-year-old. So, like any teen with big dreams and a big heart, I pivoted. I joined a girl group called "Knockout," toured around California and Nevada, and graduated high school two years early to chase music full time.

At seventeen, I went solo. My first record deal came shortly after... in Las Vegas. The label promised everything: my dream producers, big opportunities, creative freedom. I moved to Vegas at eighteen, certain I was living my dream. But dreams have plot twists. Just before my debut album was completed, the label went bankrupt.

I moved back to California, devastated and directionless. What happens when the life you built your identity around suddenly disappears?

A few months later, I saw a casting call for Hong Kong Disneyland. I auditioned on a whim with my best friend—and to our shock, we both got the job. We left for Hong Kong at nineteen, cast as "friends of" Belle, Aurora, and Cinderella. That experience changed everything. It wasn't just a job—it was the moment I began truly living my fairytale. I traveled across the world, performed daily, and created lifelong friendships. I was surrounded by magic, but I also saw how powerful it was to create it for others.

When I returned to the States, I continued performing as a "friend of" Aurora and Belle at special events for Disney until 2008. That same year, I met my husband—we married in 2012 and are still each other's favorite adventure partners. I took a brief step away from the stage to explore other paths (including becoming a certified personal trainer), but performing always called me back. Slowly, I began singing again—nursing homes, schools, churches, birthday parties. It wasn't necessarily glamorous, but it felt like home.

In 2014, I started working as a promo and trade show model. Though still living in California, I found myself in Las Vegas constantly for work, sometimes more than fifteen times a year. I fell in love with the city all over again. Vegas had a rhythm, a sparkle, a heartbeat I couldn't get enough of. Eventually, my husband and I decided to make it permanent. I moved back to Las Vegas in 2022, and I can say with certainty: it was the best decision we've ever made. There's a magic here that still gives me butterflies.

Now, I live a life that blends all my favorite worlds—performing, storytelling, travel, fashion, and creativity. My "day job" is working conventions as a lead generator, product specialist, and emcee. But my heart? It beats for the art I create with others: photoshoots at sunrise in the Bellagio Gardens, ball gowns in desert landscapes, content that feels like stepping into a storybook. Vegas has become my castle. And funny enough... the little girls at Bellagio who ask to take a photo with "the princess"? They remind me that the fairytale never really ended—it just evolved.

Like anyone who dares to dream, my path has had detours and heartbreak. But I've also learned that fairytales aren't perfect—they're just proof that something beautiful can grow from something uncertain. I've come full circle, performing again at fantasy balls and masquerade events, singing arias in gowns beneath glittering chandeliers. It's a dream I didn't know was still waiting for me. Give me a gown, good acoustics, and a room full of wonder—and I'm in heaven.

What I've discovered along the way is this: the most powerful thing you can do is be unapologetically, authentically you. You'll never please everyone, so why not dress how you want, sing what you love, and live like it's your own enchanted novel?

Dearest reader, if you take anything from my story, let it be this: your life is allowed to be magical, even when it's messy. Follow your heart, even when the path is unclear. Surround yourself with people who see your light—like I have in my husband, my parents, my closest friends, and my faith in God. You don't need permission to wear the dress, start again, or take up space. You are not "too much"—you are just enough. You don't have to wait for a special occasion to romanticize your life.

Every woman deserves to feel like she's in her own fairytale. I hope mine reminds you that you can start living yours anytime... even today.

Follow along with my story at @tawnyinwonderland. I'll be the one in the gown.

About Tawny

Tawny Triska Pollard is a performer, content creator, and modern-day fairytale enthusiast based in Las Vegas, Nevada. With a background in classical music and commercial pop, Tawny has spent most of her life on stage—whether singing Italian arias, joining a girl band as a teen, or performing as a "friend of" Disney princesses at Hong Kong Disneyland and the El Capitan Theatre in Hollywood.

After years of working in entertainment and convention industries, Tawny found a unique creative niche where all her passions collide. Known online as @tawnyinwonderland, she blends fashion, fantasy, and storytelling to inspire others to romanticize their everyday lives. Her whimsical content—often featuring dreamy gowns, golden light, and a sparkle of magic—has caught the attention of photographers, designers, and other creatives all over.

Beyond content creation, Tawny continues to perform, singing at fantasy balls and masquerades throughout the West Coast. Whether she's leading teams at conventions or bringing characters to life through music, her mission remains the same: to help others step into their own fairytale by living authentically, fearlessly, and always with joy.

She credits her faith in God, her supportive family, and her husband of over a decade for being the steady roots behind her sparkle. Today, she proudly calls Las Vegas home—a city that has become both her creative playground and her greatest stage yet.

Follow along with her adventures at @tawnyinwonderland.

Redefining Beauty While Rebuilding Myself: Building More Than a Medspa

Amanda Ralph

Everything I thought I had known fell apart the moment I found my brother's nonresponsive body. My entire plan, my hopes, my dreams—everything suddenly felt pointless while I attempted CPR, unsuccessfully. Just two weeks prior, I had graduated from nursing school. I was supposed to move back home to Las Vegas, work with my brother at his hospital, and eventually open a nurse practitioner clinic together. But in a single, heartbreaking moment, my future shattered. I felt lost, hopeless, unanchored. The grief was unimaginable. I didn't know it then, but that tragedy would become the beginning of how I would eventually leave my mark on this city, my hometown.

I was born and raised in Las Vegas, on the east side, an area full of hardworking, heart-centered people. Growing up, I dreamed of leaving. But once I moved away for college, I realized how much I missed it. I had a great family and a beautiful childhood. Academically inclined, I took advanced placement classes, became class valedictorian, and stayed involved as a cheerleader, dancer, and choir member. I thought I might become a teacher like my mom. But watching my older brother enter nursing school shifted something in me. I took a required health class in high school and found a deep love for medicine— a desire to learn more and, maybe one day, work alongside my brother.

I moved to Utah at eighteen to attend Weber State University for nursing. After my brother died, I returned to Las Vegas, crushed. Just weeks after his death, I failed my nursing boards. I'd been so heartbroken and distracted that I hadn't studied.

That season was the darkest period of my life. Even though I was still so early in the grieving process, I started feeling that my brother was showing up for me in numbers: he sent me 11:11, 19, and 59. I was unsure what my new future looked like, but these little signs got me through the constant ache. I got a job at a hospital in Las Vegas and began working on an intermediate care unit. I loved the impact I made on patients, and the team was incredible, but I quickly burned out. The system was broken. I knew I needed something different. I decided to go back to nurse practitioner school in hopes that I would be able to make a difference in a less physically demanding role.

Knowing that I needed a change, I decided to look for a different job. That's when my sister told me about a medspa that hired nurses to do laser treatments. I was instantly intrigued. I applied online and was hired within one week. Looking back, I believe it was a fateful moment. I fell in love with aesthetics immediately—the science, the artistry, the chance to talk to women all day about their beauty concerns.

But I also quickly saw the dark side. I witnessed many medspas that prioritized sales over safety and outcomes. I'll never forget one experience: a forty-five-year-old woman was being pressured into an aggressive laser treatment. When she complimented my skin, the saleswoman said, "She gets this laser all the time. If you want skin like hers, you need it." I was twenty-two. I had never even had a facial. That moment made me sick, but it also lit a fire inside me.

While completing my master's degree, I floated from one medspa to another, never quite finding a place that matched the vision forming inside me—a space rooted in education, integrity, and authentic care. I kept dreaming of a place where I would want my family and friends to go. I graduated in 2018, and my dad began encouraging me to open my own practice. I was hesitant, but he persisted. One day, we toured a fourteen-hundred-square-foot space with three treatment rooms. It needed cosmetic work, but came with the equipment and furniture I needed. It felt like a sign. I was terrified, but my dad pushed me to take the leap. I did. That first year tested me and continued to fan the fire within me.

Then COVID hit. We had just started to gain traction when the world shut down. On March 14, 2020, I delivered my first child, a daughter. Though the timing was surreal, the pandemic closure gifted me three months of maternity leave to be fully present with my newborn. When I returned to work, I came back changed. I had a new purpose: to build something meaningful. To show my daughter what was possible. And I didn't do it alone. My husband supported us financially and emotionally. Not once did he make me feel I had to choose between being a mother and being an entrepreneur. His steady belief in me allowed me to dream bigger.

We restarted after COVID with a new ambition and excitement for the future. Over the next few years, we grew steadily from $60,000 in our first year to $1.3 million in year five. We expanded our staff from four to ten. We built a team of exceptional women. It was a constant grind, and I found my purpose in the consistent, steady growth. On paper, it was beginning to look like a true success. But inside, I struggled. I constantly felt like I wasn't doing enough. I was exhausted, trying to be a businesswoman and a present mother to two young children. When I had my son in 2022, I continued to hustle, but something in me was unraveling. I was still chasing external validation—from clients, from my father and business partner, from a ghost of the girl I used to be.

In year five (2024), I reached a turning point. I realized I couldn't keep living for other people's approval. I started meditating, began manifesting, and connected with my brother's spirit in a deeper way. I began to feel his presence guiding me. I made the bold—and terrifying—decision to separate my business from my dad and run it fully on my own terms. I stopped waiting for permission. I claimed my voice, my worth, and my vision. It was a difficult and sometimes painful process, but through it I found my inner knowing. For the first time, I could sit with pride for everything I'd built. It taught me to pause, to trust, and to believe that even when I don't have all the answers, I'll always be able to find the next right step.

That's when everything began to change.

Today, I'm in the process of buying a new building for White Coat Aesthetics—a four-thousand-square-foot space that will house not only expanded services but also an educational center. It's a space that represents everything I've grown into: not just a business owner, but a leader, a teacher, a force. And do you know the building's address? 59. My brother's number. It always shows up at the most pivotal moments—his way of saying, "I'm here. Keep going." I truly believe he sent this building to me.

The road to this building ownership has not been easy, and there were moments I wanted to give up. But I've used everything I have learned in the last five years to keep going. To trust myself.

Las Vegas is my home. It has held my grief, my growth, my grit. In a city of flash and spectacle, I'm building something rooted in integrity. I'm creating ethical beauty in a field that often lacks it. I'm empowering clients to feel like enough while still embracing what's possible. And I'm showing women— especially mothers—that they don't have to choose. You can raise babies and build empires. You can feel fear and still move forward. And most of all, you can trust that your path is unfolding exactly as it should.

My story began in tragedy. But it continues in triumph. Every time I see "59," I smile. My brother is still guiding me, and I am exactly where I'm meant to be.

About Amanda

Amanda Ralph, MSN, APRN, FNP-C, is a board-certified nurse practitioner, entrepreneur, and founder of *White Coat Aesthetics*, a premier medical aesthetics practice in Las Vegas. Known for her expertise in facial balancing and her commitment to natural, ethical beauty, Amanda has built a brand grounded in clinical excellence, patient education, and trust.

With over a decade of experience in healthcare and aesthetics, Amanda has become a recognized leader in the field, offering advanced injectable treatments and mentoring aspiring injectors. Amanda is deeply committed to raising the standard of care in the aesthetics industry through safety, integrity, and ongoing education. She is an Allergan Medical Institute national speaker and trainer and is frequently sought after for her balanced approach and leadership style.

Outside of her professional achievements, Amanda is a proud wife and mother of two. She believes deeply in the power of women to lead both in business and at home, and she is passionate about showing that it is possible to build a thriving career without sacrificing motherhood or authenticity. She is a Las Vegas native and loves her hometown.

Through her work, Amanda continues to elevate the aesthetics industry while empowering women to step into leadership, own their worth, and pursue their visions without compromise.

www.whitecoataesthetics.com
Instagram: @whitecoataesthetics and @amandaralph_np

Following My Purpose

Kyra Symone

Growing up, I always knew that I was destined for greatness. I couldn't quite define it, but I felt it in my bones. Those feelings fueled my determination to work hard, excel academically, and persevere through trials. I learned early on that success required more than beauty and talent. It demanded focus, growth through adversity, the courage to establish boundaries, and the willingness to step outside my comfort zone. Once I tapped into that inner strength, I knew I was meant to leave a lasting impression on the world and leave a unique footprint that could not be erased.

Much of that foundation was laid by my parents. They instilled in me a deep understanding of purpose and helped me see that true fulfillment lies not just in enduring hardships, but in contributing to something greater than yourself. Purpose, I came to realize, is rooted in your core values and evolves as you encounter new experiences.

But nothing shaped me more profoundly than the loss of my father when I was just fifteen years old. His death was sudden and devastating. Our lives shifted overnight from comfort and privilege to budgeting and sacrifice. My mother, strong and determined, did everything she could to maintain the lifestyle I was used to. She was remarkable! But no matter how much she did, the absence of my father left a hole in me that could not be filled. That loss forced me to grow up quickly. It altered my understanding of stability and forced me to redefine what security and resilience looked like.

My entry into the nightlife industry was unplanned but transformative. What started as collecting emails for guest lists quickly evolved into booking bottle service and working for one of the top entertainment companies in San Diego. I became very influential fast, earning the nickname "Kyra San Diego." If you wanted a luxury experience in the city, I was the one to make it happen. Still, under the sparkle of club lights and VIP tables, I felt a disconnect. The glamour was real, but my soul craved depth and meaning.

That's when I knew I needed to get back to my roots, where community service ultimately anchored my life. I had been volunteering since I was fourteen, helping at summer camps, convalescent homes, orphanages, and nonprofit organizations like Feeding America, the Cancer Society, and the Juvenile Diabetes Research Foundation. Those experiences grounded me and reminded me of my deeper calling. I reconnected with my inner self not through titles or accomplishments, but through acts of service.

One evening, I had dinner with a man who mentioned he volunteered weekly with the Salvation Army. I was intrigued and joined him the following week. The impact was immediate. I felt moved in a way that nothing else in my life had evoked. I invited my best friend Lindsay to join me, and together we got involved with the local nonprofit called Urban Angels. What began as weekly soup kitchen nights soon turned into a full-fledged movement. We helped Urban Angels expand, eventually partnering with organizations like PATH and Connections Housing. The mission evolved from serving food to facilitating programs that helped people transition from homelessness to stable living. We didn't start the charity, but we helped it flourish. We were the water and sunlight that turned the seed into a blooming garden.

Despite my growing sense of purpose, my nightlife career began to plateau. I wasn't getting the recognition I believed I had earned by being offered a partnership like my male coworkers, and I couldn't help but wonder if being a woman in a male-dominated field played a role. When I was offered a position as one of the only female VIP hosts for the Light Group at a very popular club in Las Vegas, I jumped at the opportunity. Even though I would continue working in a male-dominant atmosphere, I would be working in a bigger playing field which would provide better opportunities for growth.

Known for its hustle and bustle, Vegas had a "whole different vibe." The energy was unmatched, but so were the challenges. The assumption from many tourists was that everything and everyone had a price. I was propositioned constantly by people who prejudged and misunderstood what I did and who I was. I was raised with faith and values, and I worked hard to maintain my integrity. Being constantly misjudged wore me down. Yet, I allowed nothing and no one to break my integrity.

Then, another accident changed everything again. I slipped on the job, suffering a concussion and a broken tailbone. The injury forced me to take six months off. During that downtime, I reflected on what I truly wanted. I realized I didn't want to go back. So I didn't.

Instead, I launched my own independent hosting company and modeling agency. I already had the contacts, a client base, the reputation and the skill set. My business gained traction immediately, but just as momentum picked up, the pandemic hit. Thousands of people started dying from COVID-19, and everyone was isolated inside their homes. The world shut down, including Las Vegas. Everything was paused, and like so many others I found myself out of work.

Then came an unexpected lifeline from a group chat I had started years ago with models around the country. Someone posted about a live-streaming app where people could make real money showing PG content. The best part was that you could safely stream from your home and still be able to make a living. I was skeptical. I'd always been a private person, and the idea of being live on camera felt uncomfortable. But I was more afraid of losing everything I had worked for. So I gave it a shot.

In March 2020, I began streaming on Bigo. At first, it was rough. Bigo wasn't the curated aesthetic of Instagram, it was raw, real, and live. But soon, I found my rhythm. I shared my passions: singing, dancing, painting, cooking, skincare, makeup, gardening, and grooming my dogs. People connected with my authenticity, and my following grew.

Eventually, Bigo approached me about starting my own agency. That was the ultimate turning point. I wasn't just making money, I was empowering others to change their lives too. One woman joined my agency to earn enough money to put her son through college. Within a year, she paid his full tuition and bought him a new car. Today, she is saving to buy her first home. That's the kind of success I live for. The kind that uplifts families and futures. That's the definition of success.

Today, I run one of the top agencies on Bigo Live, with over four hundred hosts. I've been featured on multiple billboards in different cities, appeared on the cover of magazines, was interviewed by celebrities at the exclusive events, starred in national commercials, and even had virtual gifts named after me. My work has appeared across multiple digital platforms, not because I chased the spotlight, but because I followed my purpose.

And still, I know I'm just getting started.

If you're unfamiliar with Bigo Live, it's a live-streaming platform similar to Twitch that features diverse content like music, fitness, cooking, gaming, art, casual conversations, and more. Unlike many other streaming apps, Bigo is primarily PG and centers around creativity and community, not adult content.

My story is still being written. My purpose is still unfolding. What remains constant is my commitment: to live with integrity, uplift others, and leave this world better than I found it.

About Kyra

Kyra Symone is a multifaceted powerhouse in entertainment and digital media. A professional model since the age of five, she has walked in tons of fashion shows, graced magazine covers and appeared in multiple television productions. As a live-streamer and social media influencer, she fuses authenticity with impact, cultivating deep connections with her global audience.

Kyra is the founder and CEO of Performing Assets Talent Agency, a proud partner of Bigo Live running one of the top agencies, with over four hundred hosts. She's been featured on multiple billboards in different cities, appeared on the cover of magazines and starred in national commercials. Through her agency, she recruits and mentors content creators, influencers, and artists. She helps them monetize their talents and build sustainable, purpose driven brands. Her work as a talent agent extends beyond digital platforms, as she actively books talent and nurtures new faces in the modeling and entertainment industry.

Based in Las Vegas, Kyra also curates bespoke luxury experiences as an independent VIP host for multiple popular nightclubs and dayclubs. She combines her network and expertise to deliver unforgettable moments for her clients.

A dedicated humanitarian, she has volunteered with convalescent homes, orphanages, and nonprofit organizations such as Feeding America, The Cancer Society, Juvenile Diabetes Research Foundation, Urban Angels, and others. Her mission is rooted in empowerment, purpose, and creating space for others to thrive. She lives by the motto, "I just want to leave the world in a better place than the way I found it."

Instagram: @kyrasymone

The Great Reset: Creating a Career My Way

Tisha Tinsman

I was born into a life most children only see in movies, a world filled with sequins, spotlight, sawdust, and wonder.

My parents were circus performers with the Big Apple Circus, so my childhood was anything but ordinary. I spent my early years living backstage in trailers, mesmerized by my mother putting on her makeup and watching my dad's handstand act from the wings, often under the supervision of Zamaratti, the contortionist, warming up nearby. It wasn't just a childhood; it was a full immersion of cultures and the performing arts.

When I was about five, my parents decided to settle down in Bucks County, Pa., while my dad recovered from an accident. I suddenly found myself with a backyard, my own room, and a consistent school routine. But the magic of performance never left me; it was stitched into the fabric of my being. My creativity found new homes in crafts, baking, and homemade projects with my mom and grandmother. If we could dream it, we could make it. If we could make it, we could gift it. That mindset would later become the heartbeat of my business, but I didn't know that yet.

As I grew, my love of dance, theater, and performance blossomed. I lived for rehearsals, costumes, stage lights, and the rush of the curtain rising. I was set on becoming a dancer professionally, until a high school injury during a musical changed everything. It was crushing at the time. When your identity is so deeply tied to your art, the thought of losing that future feels like grief.

But sometimes breakdowns are invitations to breakthrough.

As I healed, I found myself reflecting on what I truly loved most. I realized I didn't just love performing, I loved the transformation. The ritual of getting ready, the meticulous details of hair, makeup, and costume, the art of stepping into another world. That spark led me to the University of North Carolina School of the Arts, where I earned my BFA in wigs and makeup for film and theater. My time there challenged and refined me. It gave me tools, discipline, and a deep appreciation for the artistry behind the scenes.

In March of my senior year, I was offered a job on *Phantom: The Las Vegas Spectacular*. I was stunned and thrilled. The dean gave me permission to accept the offer and leave early under one condition: that I return in June to walk at graduation. It felt like my stars were aligning. I moved across the country to Las Vegas, ready to chase my dreams.

Las Vegas welcomed me with open arms and an open stage. *Phantom* was everything I hoped it would be: intense, breathtaking, and filled with seasoned professionals from all over the world. A year later, I joined *KÀ* by Cirque du Soleil as a makeup artist, and began what would become an eight-year journey with the company, working on several shows and even three full show creations. My career grew, my artistry evolved, and I was part of something spectacular every single day.

But life isn't just about what we do. It's about who we become.

Becoming a mother shook my foundation in the most beautiful, but undeniable, way. After my daughter was born, I returned to the stage, but something in me felt out of sync. The same backstage I had once thrived in suddenly felt heavy. Late-night shows clashed with bedtime stories. The adrenaline of running shows couldn't compete with tiny hands reaching for me, asking for a hug.

I realized I didn't want to miss her birthdays. I didn't want to miss Sunday pancakes or spontaneous after-dinner dance parties. I didn't want to live a life where presence came in second to paychecks.

After throwing my daughter's first birthday party, an event I went all out for, friends and family kept telling me, "You need to start a party business." At first, I brushed it off. But the idea began to grow. I started a blog, a place where busy moms could find inspiration and ideas to throw memorable, Instagram-worthy celebrations without breaking the bank. I poured my heart into it.

Soon, friends started hiring me for their kids' parties. I did it all—decor, favors, cakes, the whole nine yards. But I quickly realized something: trying to do everything wasn't just exhausting, it wasn't profitable. I was chasing a dream that was burning me out.

That's when I asked myself a powerful question: If I could choose just one thing, one part of this whole production to focus on, what would it be?

I looked at my overhead, the demand, the creative potential, and landed on something unexpected yet totally perfect: balloons.

I like to say balloons chose me. They offered color, joy, drama, art and flexibility. I could create beauty on my schedule. I could still design magical moments, but now I could do it with a clearer mind and a healthier heart.

Then COVID hit. The shows shut down. My entire former industry went dark. It was scary, yes, but in a way, it was also the push I needed. I was no longer dipping my toe in entrepreneurship. I was all in. A full-time business owner. An artist. A mother. A woman designing her life on her own terms.

When the shows reopened, they called to offer me my job back, and I felt something unexpected: peace. I was grateful, but I didn't hesitate. I told them *thank you, but I'm doing my own thing now*. And it was the truth. I had something real. Something aligned. Something mine.

That moment was more than just a career decision; it was a personal revolution. My Great Reset.

It marked the start of a new kind of ambition, one rooted in intention, presence, and purpose. I didn't want to build a business that took me away from my family. I wanted one that allowed me to be with them, that included them, that made them proud.

But something else began growing too: my love for community.

In an industry often driven by competition, I leaned into something different: collaboration. I didn't want to hoard success. I wanted to share it. I wanted to model something different for my daughters: a business where kindness, support, and generosity weren't just side values, they were core values.

Collaboration for me looks like:

- Hiring fellow balloon pros for big installations instead of doing it all myself.
- Sending referrals to other artists when I'm unavailable.
- Reaching out to local creatives for last-minute help without hesitation—and offering the same in return.

I've seen firsthand how rising together lifts us all. Creating an authentic, niche brand has given me confidence and clarity, but it's also reminded me that there's enough room for all of us.

People ask me if it's risky to help the "competition." My answer? Maybe. But I'm not building this to win alone. I'm building this to win well.

There is a deep freedom in creating a life where your work supports your values instead of conflicting with them. A life where success includes peace, where creativity doesn't mean burnout, and where showing up for your family doesn't mean disappearing from your dreams.

These days, I measure success by different metrics:

- Did I get to have dinner with my kids?
- Did I lift up another woman in business today?
- Did I create something beautiful and sustainable?

If the answer is yes, then I'm right where I need to be.

I often look back at the little girl growing up backstage at the circus. She was mesmerized by the magic, the transformation, the spectacle. And here I am, still creating magic. Still transforming spaces. Still sharing joy.

Only now, the greatest act isn't on the stage—it's the life I've built off it.

About Tisha

Tisha Tinsman is the founder and creative visionary behind Little Party Girl Co., a luxury balloon brand based in Las Vegas known for its bold, whimsical, and high-end installations. With an innate sense of style and a background rooted in the performing arts, Tisha transforms everyday celebrations into show-stopping experiences.

Before launching her career in the balloon industry, Tisha worked as a professional makeup artist on some of the Las Vegas Strip's most iconic productions, including Cirque du Soleil and Le Rêve. Her time backstage gave her a masterclass in storytelling through design, sharpening her eye for color theory, scale, and theatrical impact. That same artistry now informs every arch, garland, and sculpture she creates.

More than a designer, Tisha is a connector. She's deeply passionate about building a sense of community among fellow balloon artists and creatives in Las Vegas. Whether mentoring newcomers, collaborating with local vendors, or championing creative innovation, she's committed to elevating the industry through generosity, encouragement, and heart-centered leadership.

At the core of her work is a belief that celebration is an art form, and that even the smallest gathering holds the potential for magic. With vision, intention, and a touch of drama, Tisha brings those moments to life and makes the ordinary unforgettable.

www.littlepartygirl.com
Instagram: @littlepartygirlco
Facebook: Little Party Girl

Poured with Passion, Built with Resilience

Maria Valetta

Dedication
To my mother and father—for the love you poured into me, the lessons you left me, and the wings you gave me to chase my dreams. I raise my glass to you, always.

Some tread as though the ground were fragile glass, each step measured and silent. I prefer to pour myself into life—a glass of bold red in one hand, daring dreams in the other.

Life didn't hand me a silver dining platter. It handed me a series of heartbreaks, challenges, and crossroads. But it also gave me a fire inside that refused to flicker out—even in the darkest of times. Leaving my mark isn't about avoiding pain; it's about transforming every scar, every setback, every loss into something powerful.

If you had asked me at eighteen where I'd be today, I would've said *fashion designer,* without hesitation. I went to college for it, chased it relentlessly, and dreamed of seeing my name stitched into the back of a gown. But destiny doesn't take requests—and mine was about to uncork something much bigger.

When I dove headfirst into the fashion world, something inside me felt off. It wasn't fear. It was intuition—a quiet but persistent knowing. I realized I was meant for something else, something bigger, something rooted in connection rather than aesthetics. It took courage to walk away, but leaving that path opened every door that truly mattered. Sometimes the dreams we outgrow make space for the lives we're meant to live.

My wine journey started with a flicker of curiosity. As a young woman, I could navigate any food menu—flavors, textures, techniques—but the wine list? It was a mystery, always handed to the man at the table. I decided it was time to claim my seat at the wine table—permanently. That frustration became the spark that led me to study wine obsessively, earn prestigious certifications, travel the world's vineyards, and fall in love with the history, the people, and the stories inside every bottle.

That curiosity also changed my life in ways no degree could have predicted. I found myself hosting a wine segment called *Uncorked* for Philly.com—the Philadelphia Inquirer's digital platform—long before online video became what it is today. And through that role, life introduced me to my future husband.

Eric Grilly was the president and CEO of Philly.com. We exchanged professional meetings and polite conversations, but it wasn't until my mother passed away that everything shifted. I received flowers from his company, assuming they were from my usual contacts. But when I called to thank them, I learned they were personally from Eric. That one phone call—rooted in grief—blossomed into everything I never knew I needed.

Sometimes, I think my mother orchestrated it from above. Before she passed, she told me her greatest sadness was that she would miss the milestones of my life—my marriage, my future family. She said she would feel better "leaving" if she knew I had someone by my side. At the time, I was single. Maybe she made a little magic happen from the heavens.

Eric has been my rock ever since—through every move, every heartbreak, every new beginning.

Loss has been an unrelenting teacher in my life. I was in my twenties when I became my mother's caregiver during her battle with ALS—a disease that strips away everything with ruthless precision. When she passed, part of me shattered. Christmas, her favorite holiday, became a complicated season, layered with bittersweet memories.

On Christmas Day 2018, I lost my stepfather to suicide. Three years later, on Christmas Day 2021, I lost my father—the man who taught me the beauty of connection, the importance of friendship, and the depth of unconditional love. Grief could have swallowed me whole. But I chose to celebrate louder, love deeper, and sparkle harder.

I still honor Christmas.

I leave my tree up longer.

I cook the recipes my mother loved.

I toast not to absence, but to presence—the memories, the love, the life we shared.

Through it all, I learned a powerful truth: your greatest wounds can become the foundation of your greatest strength.

Starting over became second nature. Relocating for Eric's career meant building new lives from scratch in unfamiliar cities—new friends, new dreams, new roots. And every time, I chose to show up. Because if you want a full life, you have to build it yourself, again and again.

Some my fiercest battles were fought within my own body. My fertility journey wasn't a straight line—it was a battlefield dressed in hope. I survived two miscarriages, each one carving out a piece of my heart, but never my spirit. Surgery after surgery tried to knock me down, but I kept getting back up, fueled by the stubborn belief that my story wasn't over. A hysterectomy at the Center for Endometriosis Care in Atlanta closed one chapter, but it didn't close my future. We created six embryos with the help of an egg donor—six tiny miracles—and dared to believe in a new kind of beginning. But hope wasn't enough. The first embryo implanted—we celebrated—and then, loss. The second embryo failed to take. And then the final blow: the surrogacy escrow company stole our funds. It would have been so easy to give up—to sink into bitterness. But I didn't. Instead, I became an advocate—for fertility education, for women's health, for knowledge.

Why are we taught to chase every dream but not taught about our AMH levels, FSH, or fertility timelines until it's too late? Women deserve better. We deserve knowledge *before* heartbreak. And we deserve to trust our intuition—because no one knows your body better than you.

My story—my losses, my pivots, my passions—became my power. I believe curiosity creates magic. When you follow what fascinates you, the world opens doors you never even knew existed. I believe passion leads to purpose. When you love what you do, work becomes joy, not obligation.

I believe connection is our real wealth. It's the friendships, the late-night conversations, the laughter over shared glasses of wine that make life rich. And above all, I believe resilience is a choice. It's not something life hands you—it's something you fight for, build for, *rise* for.

I'm an only child without my parents, but I am not alone.

I have love.

I have strength.

I have a fire that refuses to be extinguished.

Leaving your mark isn't about waiting for permission. It's about daring to live boldly, to rebuild bravely, and to love outrageously—no matter how many times life asks you to start over.

I'm here to slay grief. To slay setbacks. To slay beginnings. To slay dreams that scare even me. Because the real magic of life isn't about what happens *to* you. It's about what you choose to *make* of it.

Curiosity is my compass.

Passion is my fuel.

Connection is my secret weapon.

And resilience?

Resilience is my crown.

Today I strive to work with passion, live with purpose and drink with joy.

About Maria

Maria Valetta, widely known as "Maria The Wine Blonde," is an internationally certified wine expert, food and wine writer, content creator, and private luxury wine tasting host. With prestigious credentials—including the WSET diploma and certified sommelier—Maria has transformed deep curiosity into a thriving career built around passion, connection, and education.

Her journey into wine wasn't just a career move; it was a calling sparked by a single moment of curiosity and a drive to master a field that once felt off-limits. Today, she travels the world exploring wine regions, sharing her expertise, and inspiring others to savor life's most beautiful experiences, one glass at a time.

Maria's path hasn't been without hardship. Through profound personal loss, multiple surgeries, a challenging fertility journey, and the resilience required to start over in new cities, she has crafted a life rooted in strength, authenticity, and heart. A fierce advocate for women's health empowerment, she encourages others to trust their intuition, seek knowledge early, and advocate fiercely for their own wellness journeys.

Whether hosting a luxury tasting event, writing about wine and culinary culture, or connecting with her community on social media, Maria brings a signature blend of expertise, elegance, and bold personality to everything she touches.

Her motto? *Full Glass. High Class. Unapologetic Sass.*

Instagram: @mariathewineblonde @mariatheblondesomm
Tik Tok: @mariathewineblonde
Join Maria's Wine Club:
https://my.boissetcollection.com/mariathewineblonde

About the Curator, Leigh M. Clark

Four-time best-selling author Leigh M. Clark is known for her inspiring books, including *The Dream is in Your Hands*, *Living Kindly*, and the *Slay the USA* series. Her work as an author has empowered and motivated countless readers by highlighting kindness, resilience, and the strength of community. In addition to her writing career, Leigh has over 20 years of experience as a business strategist, working with Fortune 500 companies to help them grow and succeed.

Leigh's latest project, the Slay the USA series, is a growing national movement that shines a spotlight on extraordinary women across the country who are leaving their mark on their communities and industries. Through this series, Leigh is empowering these women to share their stories of triumph, leadership, and impact, much like she has done in her own life. The series is rapidly expanding, highlighting women in cities from coast to coast, celebrating their contributions and inspiring others to follow their lead.

Leigh's expertise and passion for leadership and empowerment have made her a sought-after speaker, with multiple appearances on the TEDx stage. Her stories of kindness and personal growth have been featured in prominent publications like *HuffPost* and shared through appearances on *The Today Show* and the *Rachael Ray Show*.

As the founder of Kindleigh, a movement focused on giving back through acts of kindness, Leigh has led initiatives that have raised significant funds for charitable causes. Her mission is to create lasting change through kindness and sharing stories of impact, further solidifying her role as a leader in philanthropy.

Leigh resides in Southwest Florida with her son, Carter, and the love of her life. She's here to make an impact and leave her mark by illuminating others.

"Don't let the world change your heart. Let your heart change the world." - Leigh M. Clark

Instagram:@leighmclark @slaytheusa
www.leighmclark.com
www.slaytheusa.com

www.ingramcontent.com/pod-product-compliance
Lightning Source LLC
Chambersburg PA
CBHW071149120626
46546CB00006B/2181